Super.
Crucial.
Human

Cheryl Cran

Author of "NextMapping – Anticipate, Navigate & Create the Future of Work" and "The Art of Change Leadership – Driving Transformation in a Fast-Paced World".

BALBOA.PRESS
A DIVISION OF HAY HOUSE

Balboa Press books may be ordered through booksellers or by contacting:

Balboa Press
A Division of Hay House
1663 Liberty Drive
Bloomington, IN 47403
www.balboapress.com
844-682-1282

Because of the dynamic nature of the Internet, any web addresses or links contained in this book may have changed since publication and may no longer be valid. The views expressed in this work are solely those of the author and do not necessarily reflect the views of the publisher, and the publisher hereby disclaims any responsibility for them.

The author of this book does not dispense medical advice or prescribe the use of any technique as a form of treatment for physical, emotional, or medical problems without the advice of a physician, either directly or indirectly. The intent of the author is only to offer information of a general nature to help you in your quest for emotional and spiritual well-being. In the event you use any of the information in this book for yourself, which is your constitutional right, the author and the publisher assume no responsibility for your actions.

Any people depicted in stock imagery provided by Getty Images are models, and such images are being used for illustrative purposes only. Certain stock imagery © Getty Images.

Print information available on the last page.

ISBN: 978-1-9822-7868-7 (sc)
ISBN: 978-1-9822-7870-0 (hc)
ISBN: 978-1-9822-7869-4 (e)

Library of Congress Control Number: 2022901511

Balboa Press rev. date: 02/18/2022

About the Author

Cheryl Cran is the founder of NextMapping™, a future of work consultancy.

She is the author of ten books including *NextMapping™ – Anticipate, Navigate and Create the Future of Work* and *The Art of Change Leadership - Driving Transformation in a Fast-Paced World.* Her clients include Amazon, Allstream, Salesforce, PWC, Upwork and more. The purpose of Cheryl's work is to help leaders and teams create their 'Next' - with a people-first mindset and a strong focus on the human condition. To find out more, visit: www.nextmapping.com

Introduction

I am writing this book in the Winter of 2021. We are almost two years into the pandemic and right now there is a rise in the variant Omicron. It has been a challenging few years of upheaval, disruption and change. Prior to the pandemic, many of us must admit we were going a hundred miles an hour.

We were all running as fast as we could before the pandemic. Technology innovation was ramping up and many of us and 24/7 technology was inundating us (and still is). We were/are suffering from going too fast and having access to too much information.

Many of us were operating at the speed of technology, almost as if we were robots. Then the pandemic swept the globe, and we were collectively frozen in time. The world was on pause. The constant stop and start of the pandemic increased our stress levels. We had to recalibrate, adjust, and change. If we were willing to acknowledge it, the pandemic was the beginning of a collective awakening.

Awakening to the awareness of how fast we'd been going.

Awakening to the acceptance we all needed to slow down.

Awakening to the reality that we were becoming more disconnected from ourselves and each other.

Awakening to the realization we were given a wakeup call and a chance to switch gears.

Awakening to greater awareness around social issues and racial injustices that were kept in the shadows and now brought to light.

Awakening to the negative impact that 24/7 technology access had on our mental well-being.

Awakening to the social trend of the 'great resignation' as workers realized they wanted more of a meaningful life rather than live solely to work.

Awakening to the realization that the problems we face must be solved with a 'higher heart intelligence'.

Collectively we learned many lessons since the beginning of the pandemic. Lessons learned are only valuable when we integrate what we have learned and from there change our beliefs, attitudes, and behaviors.

It has been and is my privilege to work with leaders and team members all over the world to help positively shift their perspectives, expand their mindsets, and share new future ready skills to create a better future. For over twenty years + it's been my passion to help people excel by helping them to integrate what they have learned from the past, engage fully in the present and embrace change to create a better future.

My previous books are focused on communication, leadership, and business. This book is also about communication and personal leadership AND it's about being human. In my previous book, "NextMapping – Anticipate, Navigate & Create the Future of Work" the focus was on a 'people first' technology enabled future. The NextMapping™ book includes research that robots and AI are/will be our new co-workers. I also shared research that even though the pace of automation is increasing we are in a continued worker shortage. What is more apparent than ever is that we need MORE humans in the future of work.

The reality with where we've been and where we are going is the next needs BETTER humans! WE need to be better humans to create what's next.

It was a humbling process to write this book, it caused me to re-examine my own behaviors and to continually check in to ensure I was walking my talk. I continually asked myself, "Am I doing what I am writing about on a consistent basis?" It is vulnerable process to write a book about being a better human. At the same time, it's been an inspiring process - it has set an even higher personal standard for me to be better and do better.

I do truly believe that as we all individually commit to being a better human, we are creating a better future.

This book is structured in four chapters with the last chapter focused on the four super crucial human skills needed to be better human beings. At the end of the book there are questions and exercises to help you map out what's next for yourself, your life, and your work.

At the core of my work and in all my books, the theme is:

A people first focus AND we all need to be better human beings.

It's a very human future in a high technology enabled life -- we **must focus on 'people first' to create what's next for ourselves, our lives, and our work.**

This book is about being human, human beings AND it's about YOU!

Now and in the future, *everyone* is a leader, which means every one of us must *rise, elevate, access higher consciousness, and evolve.*

We must seek to expand our minds and hearts and commit to being the best human we can be. I am excited and inspired for what's next.

Here's to us humans!

Cheryl

Contents

"The future of humanity is it will come together in Love. This isn't just the most likely outcome -- it is inevitable. For humanity is Love personified. The will of Love, then, will naturally define our collective destiny as it was always meant to be, Ab initio."

Wald Wassermann

One

It's a Human Future

The Future of Humanity

ALL WE NEED IS LOVE. Love makes the world go around.

I questioned myself when I wrote this opening chapter. It felt vulnerable to openly declare that the future of humanity depends on love.

My previous books focused on leadership, business, communication, and technology. However, the subtle, underlying messages in all my work has always been about love through a people first focus. What's different with this book is that I am overtly sharing a 'love people' focus.

I have always had big love for people. I believe that humans are inherently good. I am optimistic about the future of humanity. Ever since I was a young girl, I have been an insatiable reader. Everything I have read and am interested in reading is about people and humanity. When I was nine years old, I wanted to be a psychiatrist. I have always been fascinated by us as humans. Why do we do what we do? What makes us behave the way we do?

Throughout my life, my professional career and in my consulting practice I find the best leaders, the best humans, and the humans I admire the most have a huge love for people! During the writing of this book, I asked myself, "How can I talk about being a better human without addressing our unique ability to love?"

The opening quote on the previous page may sound idealistic to you, simplistic or naïve, the truth is if we dig beneath the surface of why we as humans even exist, we must acknowledge we are here to love.

The Wald Wasserman quote that opened this chapter on love is aspirational and inspirational for the future of humanity.

With the ongoing disruptions of the pandemic, we've had a choice every day to decide if we are going to choose to behave from fear or love.

This quote by John Lennon says it well:

> *"There are two motivating forces: fear and love. When we are afraid, we pull back from life. When we are in love, we open to all life has to offer with passion, excitement, and acceptance. We need to learn to love ourselves first, in all our glory and our imperfections. If we cannot love ourselves, we cannot fully open to our ability to love others or our potential to create. Evolution and all hopes for a better world rest in the fearless and open-hearted vision of people who embrace life."*

At the core of becoming a better human is to love.

Jack Ma Alibaba founder, the self-made billionaire says while IQ and EQ are important the skill needed to move us forward to the future is LQ -- love quotient.

"And what is LQ? The quotient of love, which machines will never have," said Ma.

Jack Ma believes no matter how smart machines are becoming, the world's biggest and most pressing problems will be solved not by machines, but by smart humans with the capacity for compassion, understanding and, of course, love. To Jack Ma, love is the human secret weapon that will outperform machines and drive progress. A machine does not have a heart, a machine does not have soul, and a machine does not have a belief. Human beings have the souls, have the belief, have the value; we are creative, we are showing we can control the machines," he said. Ma speaks about the need to pursue a globalization that is humane.

Think of LQ - love quotient as an overarching verb - not in the narrow view of romantic love.

Love is an all-inclusive word, a big verb, it is an action and in the context of humanity it means we love ourselves, we love our families, we love our neighbors, we love our employees, we love our clients, we love our work, we love our planet, and we love our communities.

Love our neighbors means being a good citizen, love our employees means to value them as human beings, and to treat them as sacred. Love our clients means we honor and appreciate them. Love our work means we seek to work with purpose and deeper meaning. Love our planet means we love and take care of the earth. Love our communities means we connect and get involved with our community to help create local solutions.

The future is human.

Robots cannot love, nor can the emote.

Humans have the sacred ability to impact others through love in action.

Imagine what the future could look like if every one of us shifted our perspectives towards increased compassion, tolerance, inclusion, acceptance and yes, love.

Where Pre-pandemic we glorified technology and idealized a robotized future, post-pandemic we realize we all long for more human connection. We long for authenticity, we long for truth and we long for us all to be better humans.

Using the word, 'love' in the context of business would have been seen as too soft just a few years ago. Today having gone through a global pandemic, we intuitively know at the core of our lives, caring for employees, of being a good leader and caring for customers it is, love.

Being a better human means we have a love to help others, love for the planet, love to make a difference, love to share knowledge, love to share resources and love of for all of humanity.

Picture a future where collectively we leverage the best of technology to automate the mundane, therefore allowing us to spend time on becoming better humans. As we become better humans, we elevate the humane. We elevate the planet.

Picture yourself in a world where individuals have shifted from self-gain and power over others towards a future where individuals share resources, support, and power.

Imagine a world where all genders, all cultures and people of all abilities cooperate, ideate, and create solutions to make the world a better place.

I firmly believe creating a better future includes all the above imaginings and, is not only possible it's doable and it requires us to commit to be better human beings.

Companies like <u>Integrate AI</u> state 'love people' as their primary value. The CEO and Founder Steve Irvine is a former Facebook executive who envisions a future with ethical AI at the forefront and focused on doing good for humanity.

Having a 'love people' value is an example of a company leading to a technology future with a focus on 'people first', a love for people and with a focus on making the world a better place.

Workers at Integrate AI define 'love people' as follows:

"Love people by having high emotional intelligence"

"Love people by honoring the trust our customers place in us"

"Love people means we put people first *always*"

"Love people by appreciating their perspectives"

"Love people by truly valuing their differences"

I had the pleasure to interview Steve Irvine CEO and Rachel Jacobson SVP People &; Culture from Integration AI to get their input on 'love people' as a company value.

Integrate AI Interview with Steve Irvine and Rachel Jacobson on "love people":

Cheryl: Welcome Steve and Rachel, thank you for your time today. Can we start with talking about machine learning and AI and your approach to it at Integrate AI?

Steve: Yes, I realized when we founded Integrate AI that machine learning and AI is inevitable to our future. The founding story of creating our values began with the question, "what needs to be true for machine learning and AI to be a positive thing for people?". The worst version of the AI movement is that you build mass data manipulation tools, and they can be good at taking advantage of people.

The best version of the AI future is that AI has an unbelievable ability to understand people and to embed our positive human values. Ultimately it can become a positive force for people.

Our mission is this idea to accelerate machine learning in a way that maximizes the participation and the benefit of people while maintaining trust. To be honest this is a challenge right now. Ethical AI means responsible use of data. We've got to find ways to respect privacy while gathering data for effective machine learning. Our job at Integrate AI is to build the software system that allows organizations to be able to get access to the data that they need to build meaningful models that can create positive change, while maintaining trust.

Cheryl: Can you give an example of the AI dilemma you mentioned?

Steve: Yes, I can give you an example from one of the customers we're working with, now. We're working with a hospital network, and what they're trying to do is better identify a rare disease in children. The problem is that they would like to run machine learning or an AI system to pick up the patterns of the rare disease and determine if they could triage these kids more effectively and literally save lives of more kids. The challenge is that they only have a limited amount of data. They have scanners, and they'd do the scans on these children's brains. And they might have a thousand of those scans. A thousand is not going to give us enough data to pick up an informed pattern. However, every hospital has about a thousand of these cases. If you were able to go across all the collective hospitals to pool and then pull the data, then you could run this AI model. The challenge is, it's very sensitive data. Its patient data. By privacy regulation, you can't bring it together. So, how do you solve that problem? And that's what we built our software for. So, essentially, what we do is we can train models. Imagine them like little brains that sit inside of each of the hospitals. And they can communicate with our system, the big brain in the middle to make it more productive. But it doesn't ever move the data it keeps it private. In this example we have the ability of delivering a great outcome. All the hospitals, can now, do a better job of predicting the risks of rare diseases, identify the at risk kids, and ultimately get them the care they need faster. AND it doesn't compromise privacy, and it fits into the regulations as they've been stipulated. So, there is a lot of nuances we're starting to see, entering in our world of AI and machine learning.

Cheryl: Thank you for sharing an excellent example of ethical AI as it relates to healthcare for kids, can you share how you as a company came up with 'love people' as one of your founding values?

Steve: Yes, the founding team got together, and one of the first things we did is, we asked, "What do we want to stand for, as a company?" And one of the things important to us is to build a set of values everybody could lock into, and we can use to be able to make key decisions inside of the business. The most controversial, and discussed, at the initial offsite was, 'love people'. And the reason is that it sets a ridiculously high bar when you write the word, love. And we had a lot of debate about whether we felt we could live into the high bar of a 'love people' value, we asked, "Is it right to set such a high bar?" We could have said, "Consider people," or "Like people." Love is the most aspirational goal you could set for people for sure. And we knew it would be very easy for people to criticize us if we're not living up to a very high standard when we put a value like 'love people' out there. We talked about it a lot as a team. Ultimately, what we settled on was 'love people' is the bar we'd like to be held to. We felt any type of criticism we would receive would be helpful feedback for us. The aspirational value of 'love people' would be something we would have to live up to. It supports our mission around machine learning and making sure acceleration is a positive thing for people. We're really focused on narrowing the health, wealth, and wellness gaps that exist in the world and using machine learning to be able to solve human challenges. So, we knew we must love people, because it's hard to do. So, we set, "love people" as a high bar in terms of the way we need to think about building our product. It's a high bar, in terms of how we need to think of the people inside of the company, and how we consider them and think about them. That's the high bar we want to set. And we put it out there. And the people who get it, it's really going to resonate with them. And it would help us attract the people who are aligned with us, in terms of, 'love people'. That high bar matters.

Rachel: It's interesting, because 'love people' could be interpreted to mean you should just do everything for everybody all the time. I think we've been very thoughtful about our programs, policies and benefits that consider the whole employee. We talk about "love people" to include giving tough feedback or direct feedback, but doing it in a way that's really kind, respectable and helps people grow. When you think about things like parental leave benefits, that kind of thing, in technology companies, there're companies that offer some incredibly comprehensive benefits. As a very early-stage company, it's hard to do it all. We recognize it was an important thing for families, with our employees, that we did benefits in a way that we felt was going to be sustainable but also hit a level that was helpful for our employees with families. So, it's that balance of not just opening the piggy bank all the time and giving endless amounts of time off. It's about those real relationships, which is, sometimes you give tough love feedback for people. You can't say yes to everything, all the time. Communicating with transparency and respecting each other is key.

Cheryl: In this book, I talk about it as love in action. It's not just a concept. It's an action. So, if you're a leader, love in action is sometimes you must give kind, candid feedback that might not be easy for the other person to receive. It's in the how the candid feedback is delivered that is the action of love. Some people could interpret 'love people' as well as, if you 'loved people' you would treat me like family. 'Love people' is an act of mutual accountability. Love is an action in how we each communicate, and all of us being committed to serving the greater good. Love people is an aspirational goal that holds us all to a high standard of human behavior.

Steve: I think Rachel summarized it well. And one of the things that we've tried to do, is to make 'love people' part of the culture ongoing. We build it into a lot of the key processes we've got in the company. We leverage our values in our onboarding, and our recruiting process. If you get a job at Integrate AI, you're doing just as many values interviews as you are skills interviews. We are focused on having a very diverse team. And we want alignment from our workers as it relates to our values. We want to make sure that everybody believes in the same set of values. And you'll hear conversations, often, inside of the company of, how does this line up with our values of 'love people' and 'build trust'? Love people and build trust are the two most cited values that we refer to when we make major decisions inside of the company. When we have a big all-hands meeting, and we're making a big strategic decision, or we're having collaborative conversations around key people, or decisions we need to often make, somebody will go there and say, "Are we really living into our value of, love people?" or, "We have a 'love people' value here are we living it properly?"

Cheryl: I love that you integrate the values in your onboarding because let's face it if someone is not lined up with 'love people' or 'build trust' they are likely not going to succeed in your culture.

Rachel: Exactly

Steve: There's a lot of high performers we have turned away, specifically, because they were not behaving in line with our values. You know, they can be great in another company that values things differently. But, in our company, they just don't mix.

Cheryl: I talk about automating the mundane, so we can elevate the humane. Do you think we're heading there? What keeps you optimistic about where we're going with AI and robotics and automation, machine learning? Are you hopeful we're headed in a direction that is going to positively impact humanity?

Rachel: We had a masterclass, last night, and our VP of Machine Learning Products was on it. And she had this great comment. I will do my best to paraphrase her. She basically said you can't look inside someone's head and figure out why they're behaving in a biased way. When you're building algorithms, if something bad is happening, just a little bit, you can go back and look at it and figure it out. So, there's an opportunity to catch bad and turn into something good.... It's an opportunity. We get sort of hooked up on all the negative stuff. But there's some opportunity for AI to be a real force for good.

Steve: Yeah. I think that's well said. I think to your question, do I think it's possible? Yeah. How probable it is? It just depends. I think, like any amazing technological change that you see, I think what it ends up delivering, in terms of impact to the world, has a lot to do with how it's utilized and, ultimately, the use by us humans, more so than the inherent properties of the technology. I think the opportunity is massive, and the spectrum is massive. I think the same tool you can use to find this really nuanced pattern could help you save lives, or help you meaningfully change lives, is algorithmically, not that different from the algorithm you might use to target people with drone strikes, or to be able to manipulate somebody into taking an action because you know something about how they're going to react that's harmful for them, but you know how to nudge them over the line. I think a lot of it has to do with application. And a big reason why we're a company, like why we exist, is we have a strong opinion as to how we would like to see the world grab at that. We are creating technology to enable people, that see the same future as us, to be able to get there faster, to have that impact, and show it's possible, because we feel like that's the best way to be able to substantiate that change is to be able to show what it looks and feels like to live in a world where AI can be used for all these really positive purposes, and then have people want more of this. How do we enable more of that to happen? We're trying to bring it more to the forefront, and to say, "There are risks. You should acknowledge the risks. And, with full acknowledgment like any technology or scientific advancement, this could be used in bad ways." Let's just start talking about the optimistic future though and how we can leverage technology innovation for good.

Cheryl: What do you think is the future of society, from your vantage point?

Rachel: I was thinking about it more from a future of work and in the workplace. There's been, kind of, a shift that's been coming for a long time, which really is this distinction between your at-work persona, or your in-the-world persona versus your at-home, or your social time, persona. And, over time, there's been tension between people feeling like they must show up differently in their workplaces than they do at home. We talk about younger generations not really wanting to stand for that anymore and moving away from it. Certainly, during the pandemic and with 60% of the workforce working from home, there's been an acceleration towards blurred lines between work self and home self. And I think that's a great thing because I think inherently... there's a dissonance when people must show up in a way that's not authentic, and not true to themselves. And I keep seeing this come out in a lot of different ways. Sometimes, it's just simply the way people dress or act, or whatever it is. But it also includes a diversity and inclusion perspectives, people feeling the safety to be able to be their full selves and bring that, with them, into their workplaces. There's less of a barrier between the two. I think there's been an acceleration towards greater acceptance of the 'whole self'. Or people wanting to work in places where they can bring their whole selves to work. I'd love to see that continue. I think that's a positive.

Steve: I agree. On the societal piece, I would say, it depends on where you live in the world, of what the future holds. I do think, generally, we're seeing a shift to more decentralization, and more participation. I think the world, as it existed, didn't work for a lot of people, statistically. I think, generally, we're better in the world today, than we were a hundred years ago. But it doesn't mean, that's evenly distributed. I think technology has a huge battle ahead. We're starting to see the reinvention of the internet. A lot of this movement towards, what they're calling, Web3. It's really a movement back to a more open and decentralized internet, where we're not consolidating power in a few small companies. We're trying to put power back in the hands of creators, back in the hands of individuals. I think movement will continue for a while. And I think that's generally a positive movement.

Cheryl: Yes, I do believe we are entering a renaissance period post pandemic where we will notice more power to the people. We are seeing individuals rise to demand a seat at the table and I think that's a positive trend. Thank you both for your time and insights and thank you for setting the values bar for other companies to 'love people'.

===

I enjoyed interviewing both Rachel and Steve, and I was impressed by their commitment to living the value of 'love people' in their company as well as to their commitment to ethical AI.

When we look at 'love people' as a future of humanity imperative it means we are all being held to a higher standard.

Love in action unifies and is the connector bringing humans together to create and innovate.

Looking at the future of humanity we can foresee a shift in people's attitudes towards life and work in a new way. People are rethinking their values, rethinking their lifestyles, and rethinking the meaning of work.

We are living in the now, while creating our future in every moment with our thoughts, choices, and behaviors.

The future IS now.

We can either be afraid of the future OR claim our power to courageously create it.

Psychologists state when we live in the past, we are depressed, and when we live in the future, we are anxious.

The opportunity is to accept reality, be present and 'create in the now', which leads us to an exciting and fulfilling future.

We are fully alive when we heal the past and create the present and empower ourselves to handle whatever the future brings.

We can no longer look at the future through the lens of simply 'the future of work'. We are living now in a 'future of all things' as our daily reality.

The future of all things includes:

The future of society

The future of family

The future of being human

The future of work

The future of....... well, all things!

The future of society....

A recent article in Fortune magazine shared insights into how scientists are looking to nature for innovative ideas that can be applied to the future of humanity. One area of study I find fascinating is the study of starlings and how they self-organize through <u>murmuration</u>. The form of study is called 'econophysics'.

The definition of Murmuration is:

Murmuration refers to the phenomenon that results when hundreds, sometimes thousands, of starlings fly in swooping, intricately coordinated patterns through the sky

For decades scientists, in Rome have been studying the starling murmurations for clues into human group dynamics and the wisdom of the crowd. What they found is birds 'murmurate' to avoid predators. The unpredictable movements by a group of starlings has a purpose.

What scientists are looking to find out is the human application of these phenomena. The questions they are asking, "How do the actions of an individual, or small groups trigger societal reactions like social change, market crashes or crisis"? Or "How do the actions of one individual or small groups create societal changes?"

We can link the pandemic to being a crisis which created a massive disruption and as humans we have murmerated in response. Murmurations similar to the concept of the <u>butterfly effect</u>. The butterfly effect is the idea that small things can have non-linear impacts on a complex system. The concept is imagined with a butterfly flapping its wings and causing a future environmental after effect. On a human level we could link the pandemic as a butterfly that flapped its wings creating a ripple effect of human societal changes.

One example of a societal murmuration or butterfly effect is the trend of people leaving their jobs since the beginning of the pandemic. Now being termed, 'the great resignation' it is a direct result of a major disruption or event causing people to rethink, reassess and relook at how they want to live and work.

The pandemic created a murmuration or butterfly effect of individuals being afraid for their own health or the health of loved ones and therefore being more keenly focused on well-being.

The murmuration or butterfly effect of one individual or a small group making a change can create rapid societal shifts. One TikTok, one Facebook Live, one movement, one video about love in action can go viral and shift societal attitudes overnight.

There are times when I watch the news, scroll through my news feed, or watch something on social, that makes me feel a range of emotions from sad, angry, to hopeful.

My thoughts range from, "we are going to hell in a hand basket" all the way to, "wow, I am so impressed with humankind". I have found that when I am in fear based thinking my thoughts automatically go to the negative and to the worst-case scenario. I choose to focus on hope, optimism, love and a better future.

It takes mental discipline along with commitment to stay focused on love-based thoughts over fear-based thoughts.

I am very selective about what information I take in to ensure I am not getting caught up in fear-based thinking. I balance the 'regular' news with good news stories, positive research and stories of people being great humans.

When we focus predominantly on the negative, sensational, fear based or polarizing commentary, we become depressed, despondent, and feel powerless. We can feel that as a humanity we are primitive and that we are going backwards. When we focus on the negative, we struggle with what to believe or what actions to take. When we focus on the positive we acknowledge reality, we elevate our thinking and we take inspired action.

We are inundated with information both positive and negative, what's needed now is

to choose love over fear. We need the wisdom (heart/soul, logic, and discernment) to find the truth of what we hear/see and to decide what meaning we give it.

When we focus solely on negative news or negative inputs, we feel powerless to effect positive change. When we focus on positive news that includes human progress stories, technology being used for good or human kindness stories, we feel empowered, we increase our optimism, and we experience greater faith in humanity.

Change starts within us.

I was born with a love for people. I am wired for faith (spiritual) and optimism. I come from hardy stock – my French/Dutch lineage includes hard-working farmers and clergy members.

Being raised on a farm and being a farmer comes with inherent built-in faith. Our farming family had faith in every season. We had faith in what we planted, we had faith during the growing cycle, faith in the weather, and finally faith in the harvest.

My paternal grandfather was a Catholic priest who left the priesthood to marry my paternal grandmother when her husband (his brother) died. I never knew my paternal grandfather but his brother my grandfather was an eternal optimist. He didn't see leaving the priesthood as a sacrifice, he saw it as his calling to provide for my grandmother's family. He saw leaving the priesthood as an act of love. My grandmother had seven children and was widowed in her forties. I have vivid memories of staying with my grandfather and grandmother in small town Saskatchewan. They owned a care home for mentally challenged people. The amount of love and care my grandparents had for those in her care was inspiring. My grandmother was instrumental in instilling my love for people. She believed that all people had a purpose and that all people needed to be loved. My grandmother tirelessly cooked and cared for the people in her care home. My grandfather was a calm presence, he was patient, he meditated, he shared his faith in humanity with us by telling us stories.

My father was the ultimate optimist who also loved people, he believed every setback was a sign for him to work harder. I was brought up to believe in the good, the positive, hard work, and faith.

I am my grandmothers/father's daughter, in that I am a born optimist who believes all people are inherently good.

I am a pragmatic optimist in that I do not look at people and the future through rose colored glasses. I grew up with many hardships. I am optimistic despite having a difficult upbringing and through the challenges of life.

People can let us down and disappoint us, life doesn't always make it easy to be optimistic. However, given the choice to live from fear which is pessimism or love which is optimism, I will still choose love. To stay focused on optimism I have several personal strategies. A few of those strategies are to ensure I read and watch positive news.

I counterbalance the negative 'regular news' with optimistic good news via @tanksgoodnews and @ goodnews_movement on Instagram. I also follow positive technology people like @peterdiamandis author of "Abundance – The Future Is Brighter Than You Think".

My entire Instagram feed is filled with positive hashtags like #goodnews #humansdoinggoodthings #inspiration #kindness #lovepeople #thefutureishuman

Society is made up of individuals, and everyone's individual perspectives shapes how each of us shows up in our lives, our families, and our communities.

The patterns of how we were parented or the life defining events in our lives shape our attitudes and beliefs. Our attitudes and beliefs then shape our actions.

My father's mantra was, "you can do anything you set your mind to". It was ingrained in me to have a healthy dose of faith, which came from being raised in a faith-based family. I am not talking religious faith; I am talking faith in believing in a creative force bigger than and beyond our understanding as humans.

My psychological stamina stems from deep faith in the goodness of humanity, a love for people, believing I am here for a reason, surviving traumatic hardships, and working hard.

My father, a divorced man, and a single father raised me in the sixties, which was very rare at that time. My father was married three times, we moved a lot, and each time we moved, I had to make new friends, establish a new sense of security, and shift my identity.

Divorce was a rarity in the sixties and my father was not viewed favorably in our small community. I was bullied at school and called names. Even though I was bullied, and it was tough for me in school I had teachers who were supportive and helpful. I still had faith in people because even though some people treated me badly there were other people who were kind and loving.

I share my personal stories openly with you - I am not someone who had an idyllic upbringing therefor it is easy for me to be optimistic. I choose to be optimistic because I have made peace with my difficulties and am grateful for how they have shaped me.

I strongly believe that all things that happen have a higher meaning and are opportunities to grow, learn, love more, and evolve.

We are shaped psychologically by our family upbringing, our community and society. All my life events have brought me to where I am and have made me resilient. All your life events have shaped you to be who you are and have brought you to this time and this place to choose love over fear.

As we heal ourselves and our stories, we increase our capacity for love and optimism. As a super crucial human there is no one who is going to save us. We must save ourselves. We must heal ourselves. We must do the work, invest the energy, and seek to optimistically change ourselves to be a better human.

Who we are as a person influences society.

In the past few years, we experienced heightened awareness around societal inequities such as gender inequality and racial injustice brought out into the open. Issues that have been festering and kept underground have been revealed and in the past few year's events such as:

The Women's March, Hilary Clinton a female running for President, Kamala Harris a female South Asian and Black VP, the loss of black lives such as George Floyd and others and the rise of Black Lives Matters, the rise of Asian racism since the pandemic and more.

Institutions and organizations are being held to higher expectations to increase diversity. Entertainment reflects the societal attitude shifts with shows like The Morning Show tackling issues of racism, sexism, sexual discrimination, ageism and more.

We are becoming more aware of issues that have been kept underground and hidden. There is a greater awareness around the need for change.

Leaders and companies in the past have paid lip service to diversity and inclusion, today, people demand AND expect diversity and inclusion in action.

Societal attitudes shifts include people's expectations of multicultural representation in the media, in entertainment, in the companies they work for as well as the companies they buy from.

Workers expect gender equality in the workplace. More women are standing up to claim the same resources afforded men in start-ups and the workplace. Disabled people are speaking up to be included in all job opportunities and workplace promotions.

As women rise and elevate to positions of leadership and power, we are beginning to experience a shift towards a society that values equality.

If we look at the issues of today through the lens of fear, we can fall into a pessimistic or hopeless attitude. If we look at today's issues with hope (an aspect of love) we can see that it is necessary for things to devolve before they can evolve. Watching things devolve is difficult. Change is hard however we MUST step up to create an inspiring future.

If we look at the societal shifts as necessary, that change is moving us towards a new way of being we can then be part of creating a 'love' based future.

Predictions for the future of society:

While none of us has a crystal ball, one must look at the patterns of human behavior and societal shifts, to get a sense of what society can and might look like in the future.

At NextMapping, we look at the patterns in the events that have happened to identify the trends and the shifts that are being made in society.

Here are the societal changes we foresee based on our research:

Society will become more open, more inclusive, and more tolerant of individuals differences.

Society will highly value the roles of caregiver or homemaker of any gender as equal or more valuable as the breadwinner.

Education will become 'student centric' with personalized learning plans and 'real time' learning with immediate application in life and work. Educators will increase partnerships with business leaders to solve the skilled workers shortage challenge.

Businesses will shift their approach to how they view people from 'people to achieve business goals' towards 'honoring people as sacred' and integral to the success of the future of the business.

Business leaders will increase acceptance of the diverse and unique lifestyles of their workers and how work can be done accordingly.

Leaders will willingly adapt the workflow to suit the individual workers personal choices of 'how and when' they want to work.

Racial reconciliation must and will happen to acknowledge the injustices against racial minorities. Political/community leaders will focus on healing the pain of racial injustices from the past.

Women will continue to choose to become entrepreneurs, freelancers, and contractors. More women will choose not to work within a rigid workplace structure.

Gender acceptance will be the norm -- all genders will be respected as human beings and there will be support and systems to protect gender equality.

Hybrid workplace is here to stay -- workers will continue to choose lifestyle priorities when choosing who they will work for.

Virtual work is here to stay with some companies choosing to be an entirely virtual organization.

Technology innovation for good will be leveraged to help achieve an integrated society -- i.e., / we will see **ethical** facial recognition to minimize crime or drone surveillance to monitor citizen behaviors

Extremists and terrorists will be rapidly identified through social media screening of content; AI will ethically track the movement of criminals, and they will be held accountable for negative behaviors on society.

The criminal and justice system will look to solve societal problems such as an overflowing prisons in partnership with mental health.

Younger generations will continue to push for environmental solutions through technology innovation and will bring breakthrough ideas to help solve our climate crisis.

Fake news and the truth will be 'fact checked' by ethical AI and new jobs will be created for people such as 'truth fact checkers'.

There will be an increase in urban and rural migration between states/provinces/countries as people seek to live in locations that align with their desired lifestyles.

More people will choose 'flex work' and will start their own businesses.

More people will have 'side hustles' to support flexible work lifestyles and augment incomes.

Greater acceptance of mental health and what it means to be mentally healthy and how to support those who are struggling with their mental health.

Greater acceptance and access to well-being strategies such as therapy, mindfulness, meditation, nature bathing and other holistic wellness modalities.

Greater connection with our 'local' communities as we collectively value the environment and support local.

Love in action will be the new normal as individuals and groups shift their mindsets from 'me to we'.

The future of families:

When looking at societal patterns, we observe that societies are a collection of families. In the past, family was defined with a traditional definition, which was a family that consisted of a mother, father, and children. Families today can have two mothers, two fathers and many variations of dynamics that determine a family.

Over the past decade, we have been noting massive mindset shifts about the diverse versions of family.

Today, how we describe families has expanded. Families can come in all forms, and there is growing acceptance of broadening the definition of family.

I am a fan of Glennon Doyle's work, and her book "Untamed" is a must read, she shares her journey of shifting away from societal expectations of how to live life. She tells her brave story of creating a new definition of family. I highly recommend you follow her on Instagram and read her books on humanity, tolerance, and making choices aligned with your heart, rather than on what society has set as 'normal'.

If we look at current family patterns in society, we can get a sense of the future of families:

Increased acceptance of all genders within families.

Increased value on people choosing what's best for the 'family'.

Increased awareness around 'shame' in a family and active focus on healing.

Increase in autobiographies, stories, and media coverage on the myriad types of families (adoption/birth/people we choose to call family).

Greater inclusiveness around what it means to be a 'mother' or a 'father' today.

Greater participation and less stigma about mental health including therapy, and family therapy.

Increase in community and local solutions to help families deal with family members who are struggling with mental well being.

Increased awareness by younger generations on psychology, they will have higher expectations that family members are 'woke.'

Movies and entertainment showing diverse families.

Increasing number of celebrities openly sharing their authentic selves and their real-life version of family.

Greater parental influence on schooling (including an increase in homeschooling and greater parental influence on the subjects' children learn in school).

Greater expectation of 'loving behavior' within a family which includes tolerance, acceptance, support, positive feedback, and accountability.

Based on the above patterns, we can discern that we are heading towards much greater acceptance of diverse versions of family. We will focus more on tolerance and understanding within our own families.

When you think about the evolution of families in society, we have come a long way from the days when families kept secrets and did not 'air their dirty laundry'. The denial and avoidance of truth within families has created individual toxicity, mental stress, and dysfunction. The secrets families kept created repression and denial of issues (racism, bigotry, sexism, misogyny) in society.

Today we hear more and know more about the importance of mental health. We are more aware of the negative impact of NOT addressing the truth. Celebrities like Lady Gaga and Prince Harry have helped remove the stigma of mental health struggles. People from all walks of life are much more comfortable having an open dialogue about the truth of mental health and dysfunction within families, rather than to suppress and deny it.

Based on the above patterns of increasing family openness, authentic sharing, and less stigma and shame of being human, we can peek at the potential future of families:

Families will increasingly see the value of everyone in the family getting the support and resources each person needs to be their healthiest version of self. This includes normalizing therapy as a resource to better overall mental well-being.

We will see more families choosing to live in closer proximity to each other or an increase in two families with joint living arrangements. i.e., /in- law suites or parental suites for aging parents.

An increase in social support for aging people.

Increase in options and resources to help families with aging family members.

Families will embrace the diversity of genders among all members of the family and focus less on 'gender specific' expectations.

Families will be more accepting of all viewpoints even when there is disagreement.

Families will hold each other more accountable to negative behavior - it will be normal for a teenager to call out a grandparent for an inappropriate (racist/sexist) remark. (In the past we might have stayed silent to keep the peace but by staying silent it created toxicity and resentment.)

Families will encourage everyone in the family to learn to consistently communicate openly and honestly.

Families will go into business together (this is a throwback to the fifties).

Families will choose to live in countries, states, provinces, or states where they feel the environment supports the lifestyle and well-being of the family.

These insights into the future of family are shaped by the individual attitude shifts happening. For example, you may have a family member that has been judgemental of another family member's choice in the past. However, now and in the future, there will be less judgment of a family members choice.

The impact of the pandemic on families has been immense. Parents have had to home school, kids have had to adapt to virtual learning, and families were quarantined together.

Generation Covid (Gen C) is anyone under 20 who has lived through the pandemic. The Gen C generations experience of the pandemic will influence the next version of workplace and society. Just like Gen Y influenced the technology age and the flexible workplace. Gen C will influence the future of work structures including an expectation of virtual only jobs. A Gen C who has gone to school during the pandemic has unique perspectives and distinct individual thoughts, experiences, and viewpoints about the future of their life and work.

Gen C is a generation that has been going to school virtually, watched their parents work virtually, and expect the future as virtual. So, it stands to reason that Gen C's view of the future of work is that it will need to be human centric with 'virtual and remote work'.

The future of being human....

"You can put limits on technology, but you can't stop human evolution."

The pandemic was/is a major disruption that has caused people across the globe to go through an existential crisis and to ask themselves weighty questions.

Prior to the pandemic in 2019, I had a great interview/dialogue about the future of being human with Marc Porat, founder of

General Magic and subject of an award-winning documentary. Marc is known as a passionate visionary around society, politics, economics, and technology. Marc is one of the original Apple employees and his team was responsible for the innovation that led to the creation of the iPad and iPhone. Here's a brief excerpt from my discussion with Marc (you can listen to entire discussion here):

Cheryl: When I watched the General Magic documentary, I was inspired by your human centered leadership approach and how you created such a passionate and driven team ' can you share how you did that?

Marc: The vision our team had of creating something completely revolutionary lined up with the Apple energy of relentless innovation. That passionate vision united us. Everyone on our team was incredibly intelligent and self-motivated, it was an honor to have them as human beings on the team. I knew my job was to simply harness the positive energy and intelligence of the team. All our people on the team went off and did amazing things beyond our project. There was high mutual respect among us, and we truly 'loved' each other as human beings.

Marc went on to share that the people on his team were all very interested in the future of humanity and being accountable to taking their roles of creating innovative technology for good.

Today because of massive disruptions such as the pandemic, increased natural disasters, and technology innovation we are being challenged to be better humans.

We all have have been asking ourselves deep existential questions, such as:

What is most important to me at this stage in my life?

What are my priorities?

What do I value?

Why do I work where I work?

How much work is too much work?

How much money is enough money?

What is the impact of my work on my family?

Am I compensated fairly for my work?

How do I want to be remembered?

What would it look like to live my best life?

What's best for my family?

What are my beliefs?

What activities feed my soul?

Am I doing what I love?

What would I love to do for work?

Who am I?

The deep questioning we have all been doing is part of our evolutionary growth. A global pandemic was enough of a major disruption to our lives to cause us to pause and revisit our values, and how we live our lives.

The sheer nature of the questions we are asking ourselves has caused many of the values shifts we are noticing now in ourselves, our families, and societies.

One of my former clients was a top performing CEO when the pandemic lock down happened, she noticed that when she stopped her pre-pandemic frantic pace, she became acutely aware that one of her children was struggling more than she realized with school. As a parent, she felt bad that she had been moving so fast that she missed some of the signs of her child struggling.

She brought this up in one of our coach sessions, I asked her some questions to help her determine her next steps with her newfound realization. I asked:

Why do you feel the need to always be 'doing'?

Is your work supporting what you want for your family?

Those two questions created the opportunity for her to look at her 'why'.

What she decided was that she needed to adjust her work to support her vision of what she wanted for her life and for her family. Her vision was more freedom and flexibility in her work so that she could spend more time with family.

She is part of the 'great resignation' trend, where she quit her job without knowing where she was going to land. The result of her quitting her job was immense freedom. It gave her time to reset and refocus on what she wanted for herself and her family. After a few months she was offered a remote work role where she could have more flexibility and ability to be more present and available to her kids.

We can appreciate that the workplace needs to be humanized, and it has needed this for a while. In 2015, I published my book, _"The Art of Change Leadership - Driving Transformation In a Fast Paced World"_, in it, I outlined major trends including the trend that workers would be expecting a lot more from their leaders and workplace.

Our 2015 research found workers wanted more flexibility and had higher expectations of their leaders. Fast forward to 2021 and beyond and we are in 'the great resignation'. Workers want great leaders, and they want a great place to work. The pandemic accelerated the trend of workers seeking work that fits in with their life. Rather than live to work the shift is work to have a life.

Gone are the days when a leader hired a warm body to do a job, lay out a job description and expect people to be happy to have a job.

We are in a 'workers market', which means there will be a continued shortage of workers until at least 2025, and likely 2030. It's predicted in 2022 that the great resignation will continue. A worker's market means that workers will continue to choose where they will work, how they want to work and how much they want to work.

You may have viewed the recent Amazon commercial, where people say, "I want to work two days a week WITH benefits" or "I want to work four hours a day" etc.

We are in a customized workplace reality where work is built around an individual's strengths, monetary needs, and lifestyles. A human future means leaders and organizations no longer treat workers as 'talent' that serves the business.

A human future means ALL human beings are treated with love, respect, empathy, and appreciation. A human future is where we ask what workers want in consistent ongoing surveys/polling/gaming, and we make immediate adjustments and changes based on the responses.

A worker's market means that workers who add value, produce, collaborate, and innovate at the speed of change will have the power to ask for what they want and get it.

The future of being human in the future of work is that WE ALL must be committed to becoming better human beings.

The future needs YOU, because technology can automate the mundane, and it can increase the speed of how work gets done, AND its us as human beings who have the power to connect and create context.

My predictions on what it means to be a better human:

Being a better human means being better at relationships!

Being a better human means that we value *people first*, and we leverage technology as an enabler toward creating greater human connection and collaboration.

Being a better human means we must be accountable to our behavior and its impact on others.

Being a better human means we must increase our emotional intelligence, which includes empathy, kind candor, the ability to have crucial conversations, and the ability to coach and mentor others.

Being a better human means opening our minds to be more inclusive in our thinking.

Being a better human means increasing our understanding of psychology and why people do what they do.

Being a better human means being mindful of what we say, and how we say it.

Being a better human means taking the time to share what you know, to help people grow and to watch people succeed beyond us.

Being a better human means we use social media and technology for good.

Being a better human means being humble, authentic, vulnerable, and real.

Being a better human means we take things less personally and seek to understand ourselves more deeply.

Being a better human means we wake up each day as a lifelong learner. Our daily mantra is, "what can I learn today?".

Being a better human means we no longer view each other as our 'roles', but that we recognize that we are all human beings with souls.

Being a better human means we become acutely aware of our biases and hold ourselves to a higher standard of ensuring our biases do not shape our actions.

Why We Need You

The 'next' needs you. The future needs you. The world needs you. The next needs US!

I say this as truth and inspiration, and if we are going to create a future of our own design, it starts right here now with you and me.

The next needs us to step up and meet our challenges as opportunities to creative problem solve.

The next needs us to view conflict as an opportunity to learn more about ourselves and diverse opinions.

The next needs us to stay focused on being human as our key value as we continue to innovate through technology.

The next needs us to be better listeners.

The next needs us to join, to ideate, to iterate and to create the future.

The next needs us to focus on what we can control and lead change.

The next needs us to step up for what we believe, share our insights, and speak up when we see or hear injustice.

The next needs us to help our children and grandchildren speak up and share their ideas on how we can make a better future.

The next us to systemize the predictable, so we can humanize the exceptional.

The next needs us to be the solution, and to spend less time polarizing, blaming or judging, and more time on innovating.

The next needs YOU, because there is only one of you!

Your humanness, your personality, your energy, your vibrancy, your ideas, your insights, your courage, your heart, we NEED YOU!

The future of humanity NEEDS US AND IT NEEDS YOU!

"These things will be hard, but then you can do hard things"

Glennon Doyle

Two

A Learn Mindset

CHANGE IS TOUGH, AND AS Glennon says on the previous page quote, "we can do hard things".

The past few years have had a lot of upheaval. In the past two years, we have been stretched, stressed, and challenged, and yet we have also grown. It is helpful to look at challenging situations through the lens of what we are learning.

With a 'learn' mindset, we seek to find the meaning behind life events, and to build mental resilience.

This quote by Peter Diamandis the author of "Abundance ' The Future is Better Than You Think", has this to say about mindset:

"Our mindset is everything: what one person sees as a crisis; another person sees as opportunity. The magnitude of economic and social disruption caused by COVID-19 (25% of small businesses have closed, bankruptcies are up 26%) means that many existing business models are being upended. In some cases, entire industries. As a human, you should be asking yourself: What have I learned and what challenges or problems can I solve?"

For many of us, the lessons learned because of the pandemic include:

We learned that we have absolutely zero control over many things

We learned that we have full control over our thoughts and behaviors

We learned that we could work remotely and virtually

We learned that we could spend more time with family

We learned that commuting for the sake of commuting seems quite silly now

We learned that we are all human beings

We learned that there are major inequities among us

We learned that we need to be better humans

We learned that a worker shortage means we NEED humans more than ever

We learned that we need to be more empathetic

We learned that we need to be more tolerant

We learned that we need to be more flexible

We learned that life is too short

We learned that technology can be a force for good and it can be weaponized to create polarity

We learned to deeply value who and what we love most

We learned that bad things happen and the only thing we can control when they happen is our response to those things

We learned that when things are hard, at the same time positive things and many new things are created

We learned that love is an action, and we all feel our best when we take loving action

We learned how to use Zoom, MS Teams, and all kinds of virtual platforms.

"Your meeting's over. You can relax your Zoom Face now."

What else did you learn?

Exercise:

Take a pause here to sit with the above list, and then add what you have learned in the past few years.

How did what you learn help you make some life changes?

I personally learned many things throughout the past two years that caused me to make significant decisions that positively impacted both myself and my family.

My 'learn' mindset pandemic story....

Prior to the pandemic in the Fall of 2019, I was running as fast as possible, I was traveling a lot I had major client commitments. I was burning out from the pace. As a self-employed consultant, I've always been intently focused on growing the practice. I had been through burnout before and knew the signs I was on my way there again.

My husband had had a revision surgery in December 2019 from a previous surgery that went awry, and he was scheduled for another surgery in February 2020.

Our daughter was expecting her second child in January 2020 and was having a difficult stressful pregnancy. Her first child, our granddaughter Olive was going to be soon to be heading into kindergarten. Our daughter and her husband were thinking about getting Olive into the right school where she could thrive.

Our daughter gave birth to our grandson Austin on January 22nd, 2020. When he was born, he had to spend time in the natal intensive care unit for a while because his lungs needed help for him to breathe. Our daughter and her husband slept at the hospital for a few nights while Olive stayed with us for part of the time and her Oma for the rest of the time.

My daughter and her husband took Austin home, and at nine days old had to rush him back to the hospital. At the hospital the doctors determined that Austin needed immediate open-heart surgery to repair a congenital heart defect. It was a life-or-death situation. It was extremely traumatic for my daughter and son-in-law and Olive.

Waiting for Austin to come through that surgery was agonizing. It did help that his surgeon Dr. Ghandi was known as one of the best children heart surgeons in the world. I am happy to say that the surgery was a success and today Austin is a vibrant, exuberant, and very active toddler who turns two in January 2022. To this day sharing this story my heart just wrenches and reminds me of the trauma my daughter, her husband, and my granddaughter went through.

What that experience reminded me for a second time in my life was that life is short, and it is very precious. The near loss of Austin reminded me of when I was twenty years old and my father died, he was forty-three and died of a heart attack. When my father died, I had my first realization then that life was short. The life-or-death family challenge with Austin, was a stark reminder of what is most important in life.

Going through the health crises of my husband and the 'life or death' experience of my grandson a few months before the pandemic caused me to reflect deeply on what really mattered.

You've heard the song lyric by Kelly Clarkson, "what doesn't kill you makes you stronger"? I think that lyric has held true for all of us over the past few years of living through the pandemic.

Going through my personal challenges increased my empathy and compassion for others. I found a greater ability to be more present and available in my relationships and with my clients. Earlier, I shared parts of my my upbringing and how it shaped my thinking. One of the key mental resiliency factors I use to help me stay focused on optimism is to have a 'learn mindset'.

The 'learn mindset' is a level in the 'me to we 'mindset model I created ten years ago. I developed the model to help people identify where their mind is at and to help them elevate their thinking from personal/blame (me) to a learn/share mindset (we).

The 'me to we model' is one of the daily tools I use to keep myself accountable to a learn mindset through personal disruptions. I also use the model with coach clients to navigate through their disruptions.

The 'me to we' model is simple, yet powerful.

The four mindset levels in the model are:

Personal (me level - you are focused on yourself personally).

Blame (me level - you are focused on excuses and blame).

Learn (we level - you seek to find meaning and to learn).

Share (we level - you seek to collaborate/share/elevate).

As a mindset model, 'me to we' is a tool that helps us be accountable to our thoughts and behaviors. It is also a tool to help us coach others on our teams or remind our colleagues of 'where we are focused' in our mindset and in our behaviors.

I learned a lot through the life and work events of the past few years. I felt vulnerable and helpless. In. my work I pride myself on making things happen and getting things done. My husband's health challenges, and my daughter's family crisis made me feel helpless and powerless. I learned to be more compassionate, I learned to be more understanding and I learned more about what it meant to love.

I spent time questioning my 'why's', and it caused me to ask deep existential questions. My spiritual faith and optimism helped me to know that there was something to learn throughout these experiences. I chose to stay in the 'learn' mindset from the 'me to we' model.

The questions I asked myself in alignment with 'me to we' mindset model were:

What have I learned from each experience?

What do I value the most, and are my actions aligned?

What is the best way to support my husband and his health?

What is the best way to support my daughter and her family?

Why do I take it personally when things happen out of my control?

Who and what do I blame for my stress?

Why do I believe I must work so hard that I am burning myself out?

What is my true definition of wealth?

What do I want my legacy to be?

What makes me feel my most peaceful and relaxed?

What's best for me and my family?

How much money is enough money?

How can I share what I am learning to help others?

Given my life and the pandemic what matters most to me now?

When I got quiet and practiced my daily meditation my answers to these questions came to me and revealed significant revelations.

One day in April 2020, after my morning meditation, I opened my eyes, and I had a huge rush of energy and insight that it was time to make big changes, that our family had the opportunity to make big changes and it felt urgent.

At first, I was afraid of the insights because I knew that the changes that we needed to make were going to create further disruptions. I also reminded myself to trust that any time I've had insights to make change and had the courage to take action that things always turned out in the end.

My question about 'what's best for me and my family' reminded me of previous conversations we had been having as a family about the future. My husband and I had talked about having more space and a yard. My daughter and her husband had talked about a move out of the city to live in a home with more space. My daughter and I are very close, and we wanted our families to continue to live near each other so that we could spend quality time together.

When I had asked myself the pivotal question of what's best for our family, I remembered those previous discussions about the future. I was able to remind my husband, my daughter and son-in-law about those discussions and that **now** was the time for us make a significant move.

One of the major trends due to the pandemic is both urban and rural migration. During the pandemic, record numbers of people decided to move to larger homes with offices. Others migrated from one urban city to another. Cities in Canada, such as Halifax, have had a huge population increase from other provinces where people would sell a condo in Ontario, for example, and gain a roomy house with land in Halifax.

In the US, interstate migration has increased, with Californians moving to Texas for example, in record numbers to smaller cities like Austin and San Antonio.

So, after I opened my eyes from that meditation April 2020, I knew that it was time for a big move, I remembered our daughter saying a few years before they would love to move to the Sunshine Coast in BC.

I talked to my husband and daughter and son-in-law about moving to the Sunshine Coast right away they were on board, they were excited to make the big change.

Reg was looking forward to moving from the city to the country and to have a yard and garden again. He knew his health would benefit from living in a more peaceful environment.

Our granddaughter Olive was entering kindergarten in the fall of 2020, and it was good timing for them to move before the summer. Austin was doing well post-surgery with a positive prognosis. Our daughter and her husband had mentioned before that they wanted Olive and Austin to grow up in a smaller community environment with a house with yard, and to live within walking distance to an elementary school.

We began researching properties online on the Sunshine Coast. And so, in the middle of a pandemic, we listed two properties for sale, in Vancouver. In their online research, our excited daughter and her husband had already found a house they loved. They were both working full time jobs and with two small children, couldn't get away to view the house, so my husband and I went to view the property.

We face timed them from the property, while we walked around the house and toured the school across the street. That same day they made their offer from that virtual tour and bought the house. They moved in June 2020, a few months before Olive would start kindergarten in the neighborhood community school right across the street from their new house.

Once they found their home, my husband and I made more visits to the coast to find ourselves our home. We found a home that we loved, the home had room for offices, and the grandchildren to play but it needed major work. At our age and later stage in life, rather than downsize we up sized to a four-bedroom home. We were reversing the norm, we were following the trend of more space, so we upsized to a home with space for virtual work and extra room for family.

We loved the location, the peacefulness and privacy, so we made our offer and purchased our new home. We moved in July 2020, and in September 2020 began a major renovation. While the upper level was demolished and renovated, we lived and worked through the renovation in the lower level.

I will admit that living in the house during the major renovation was extremely disruptive and stressful. A renovation in the middle of a pandemic is no joke. I will also admit I was not always my best version of being a better human during that time. However, our timing was fortuitous in that we were able to secure trades and supplies prior to the supply chain and trade worker shortages that followed.

Our home was fully renovated relatively quickly in the middle of a pandemic and by mid-January 2021 our renovation was complete. Every single day, we comment on how much we love our home, and how much we love the lifestyle for our daughter and her family. We are inspired to live here, and we love our community.

I recognize that making big changes and taking fast and drastic actions as we did is not for everyone. There were times throughout the process that were extremely stressful. What kept us going was knowing that we were making a positive change for a new future. To this day both of our families say almost daily, 'this was the best thing we ever did'.

Olive is thriving in her school, and Austin is a mini farm boy. To see my family be so happy and thriving has been worth all the previous few years of stress.

I am fortunate to continue working with my clients virtually, which I had already started to do prior to the pandemic, AND now I also get to live and work in the inspiring countryside.

Animals visit our yard daily, we have regular visits by a family of deer, there are eagles' nests nearby, hummingbirds, and occasionally, a black bear. If you follow me on Instagram @ cherylcran I am regularly posting pictures of visiting wildlife.

In September 2021, my business travel started again, and rather than feel stressed by the travel I look forward to coming home to the peaceful countryside. I enjoy going to the city where I work in studio for virtual events. I enjoy traveling for in person events, and I feel grateful when I get home. I shared this personal pandemic story with <u>Spirituality and Health</u> magazine, and it was published in their December 2021 edition.

One of the questions the interviewer asked me was how I was able to trust that it was time to make a major change. I told her that I have meditated for years and attended Deepak Chopra's Synchrodestiny meditation retreats over the years. What I have learned is to listen closely to the signs we are given to make change. I have also learned to look for signs and confirmation along the way. Meditation is one of my self-care resources that help me to say calm, centered and free from fear. I share some meditation resources with you at the end of the book.

I hope my pandemic change story resonates with you.

I know that you too have made changes in the past few years.

Maybe you are ready to make big changes now.

You might be asking 'how' to make the changes you want.

To make change you must be willing to get comfortable being uncomfortable. In working with my clients over the past few years, I know that everyone has been asking themselves the same existential questions that I had asked myself.

There are many gifts of disruption and change IF we are willing to ask the questions AND listen to the answers, that can help us decide what we need to do to create our future.

Change can be painful when we ***don't pay attention or listen*** to the changes that we need to make. Change can be painful when ***we resist*** making a change that we know will be better for us.

Choices And Consequences

Another tool I use to help my clients through change in addition to the 'me to we' model, is the "accept it, change it or leave it" model.

It's likely you have used the 'accept it, change it, or leave it' process without consciously knowing you were in your life. Likely more than a few times. Think about any change you've made, whether it's changing a relationship status, loss of a loved one, moving, changing jobs/work or kids growing up.

Before making any change, we all go through a psychological process. We vacillate between acceptance, making change and letting something go.

Here's an example of how to use the 'accept it, change it, leave it' model.

Before making a change, you would spend time trying to 'accept' things as they are. Maybe you want to change your job because you don't like your boss. Maybe you keep convincing yourself that your boss will get better or change.

Or maybe you've been doing the same work for years, and you long for something more challenging or meaningful. Maybe you are afraid to change your current job because it has become comfortable. Or maybe you feel trapped by 'golden handcuffs' the income, benefits, or holidays you receive.

In the 'accept it' stage of change, we accept our 'excuses', we accept the things that we cannot control, and we accept reality as it is.

Accepting change is a powerful choice because it brings us a sense of peace. For example, if you truly accept your reality, you no longer fight reality, you no longer moan or complain about it, and you relax into your choice to accept. If you accept that you haven't changed jobs because you like how much you are paid, your benefits and your holidays that's ok! It's the act of accepting and owning our choices that sets us free and makes us feel more peaceful.

However, if you've gone around in circles or stressed out trying to accept something, or you are tired of your excuses and continually feel unsettled, or unhappy, then you move to the next stage, which is 'change it'.

Let's use the same example of changing your job with the 'change it' choice. When you make the 'change it' choice, you accept that which you cannot change. You accept that your boss will never change, and we can't change other people (although many of us continue to hope they will).

You can't change the patterns or the facts, for example the company culture will never change. Or your boss's boss will never change.

The 'change it' choice is a full stop accountability crossroad.

When we get to the 'change it' choice, we focus on what we can control. We CAN change our mindset, we CAN change our attitude, we CAN change our skills, we CAN change our behaviors, we CAN change the way we communicate, we

CAN change how we approach a problem, and we CAN change ourselves.

When we are at the change it crossroad in our lives, we can focus intently on upskilling our communication, we can focus on trying a new approach with our challenge, and we can take full accountability for clearly committing to the outcome we are seeking.

Again, using the above example of changing your job your 'change it' approach could be:

You shift your mindset from feeling victimized by your leader or circumstance towards feeling empowered to speak up.

You shift your attitude from negative expectations towards positive outcomes.

You acknowledge your excuses and own the 'comfort zone' reasons why you stay.

You read, watch, and learn how to communicate your feelings, needs and desired outcomes.

You create a pros and cons list of what you like about your job and your leader and what you don't like about your job and your leader.

You reach out to HR or a confidante for advice and support on the best approach to have a conversation with your leader.

You muster up the courage to set up a crucial conversation with your leader about your challenges while also proposing solutions.

You clearly articulate what you would like to create in the future.

You honestly share your challenges.

You envision the perfect job with the perfect leader.

Please note that if you cannot take ownership of the change actions such as the ability to muster up the courage to approach your leader you will be stuck between the 'accept it' and 'leave it' choices indefinitely.

"In my experience, a lot of people wait for the other person to change. I've had many coach clients who have said, "but HE or SHE is the leader they SHOULD be the one to change first".

My response is to point out that expecting others to change without communicating to them is both the 'personal' and 'blame' level from the 'me to we model. As soon as we expect what others 'should' be doing we are shoulding on ourselves and when we tell others what they 'should' be doing we are shoulding all over them!

There is no doubt that both the 'accept it' and the 'change it' choices are super difficult. It takes a deep commitment to do something about being 'stuck' and to take action to lead the change you want to be and see.

It takes profound courage to speak up and schedule crucial conversations even though we know it will be uncomfortable.

What I've found is when I've the humility to 'accept' things as they are, I relax, and I stop fighting with reality. There is a wonderful book and free online resources by Byron Katie, titled, "Loving What Is" that has helped me and some of my clients with the 'accept it' choice. In fact, Byron Katies work has been pivotal in helping to accept past events including the sudden loss of my father when I was twenty.

When I see the signals that it's time to 'change it', it means I must be vulnerable to express my thoughts, feelings, and desired outcomes to those involved. I know it's time to make the leave choice when I've tried and tried to accept a situation, tried to change myself and my approach and nothing has changed.

The 'leave it' choice does not happen until we've exhausted our attempts to accept and be accountable to change. Ultimately, if we cannot accept it and we have done everything in our power to change it, then it's time to leave it.

Exercise:

Pause here and reflect about a major life event or a recent challenge you've had, and overlay the three choices of accept it, change it, or leave it on your event.

Did you make all three choices?

How long did you vacillate between 'accept it' and 'change it' before ultimately making the 'leave it' choice?

Most of us will not make the 'leave it' choice lightly, and in some cases many of us will procrastinate the 'leave it' choice because it's a frightening and can be the most life disruptive choice.

For example, let's use my personal pandemic story to overlay the three choices:

Accept it choice: The pandemic hits and affects my life and business. The pandemic was the third major disruption for me after my husband's health, my grandsons' life or death issue, and then the pandemic hit. The trifecta of these events caused me try and accept my situation. I was integrating the reality that I had no power to help my husband and no power to help my daughter and her family. While spending time in the accept it choice I spent a lot of time journaling and there were lots of tears. I reached out for support from my coach and our family therapist. My business was going to be changing for the unforeseeable future. I would not be traveling, and my work needed to transition to virtual full time immediately. I asked myself existential questions in the 'accept it' stage. I meditated on the existential questions daily to gain insights, clarity, and answers. The answers to my questions that came to me helped me to determine if I could 'accept' it or was it time to change. I determined that I could accept that I had zero control over life and death. The daily pandemic reporting was emphasizing that we had no control over the events that were unfolding. I could accept the things I could not control AND there were things that I could change.

Change it choice: As a result of asking myself the existential questions and meditating on the answers it was clear to me that I could change my perspective about the pandemic and see it as an opportunity to make major changes. I could change how I was going to run the business (virtual indefinitely). I could focus on staying optimistic and hopeful rather than buy into the mass fear. I could change the lifestyle for my husband's well-being, for my own well-being and for my daughter and her family's well-being. I could envision a better way of living for myself and my family. The events that had happened in my life were all signals that it was time to make a change. I imagined and visualized what it could be like to live in a smaller community; I shifted my focus to imagine the lifestyle in the country versus the city. From there I decided to talk to my family about the timing to make a major change of selling/buying a total of four properties and moving to the Sunshine Coast.

Leave it choice: I had spent time on accepting the pandemic reality as is, then I spent time changing my attitude/mindset/actions to make change. We took the actions of listing properties, finding properties, moving, renovating, and all that goes along with those actions. Then ultimately, we left the city for the country to live a new lifestyle and reality. Leaving the city was an adjustment, we had lived in the city for over thirty years. However, I kept focusing on the new vision for the future, how

I wanted more peace, how I wanted a simpler life and how I wanted a better quality of life for myself and my family. We left the conveniences of the city such as Door Dash and Uber. We gained more healthier home cooked meals and a slower pace.

With every change we encounter, we have choices.

With every choice we make, there are consequences.

As human beings, we must become even more aware of our power to choose, and equally willing to accept the consequences of our choices.

The next needs us to be 'change leaders' and to bravely make change.

The next needs us to own our choices at the highest levels of integrity.

The next needs us to ensure our choices align with what we value.

If we value healthy relationships, we will make choices out of love.

If we value love and connection over being right, we will make choices that are heart centered and aligned with our soul.

If we value human beings, value connection and value collaboration, we will make choices for the higher good of ourselves and those we interact with.

"Some changes look negative on the surface, but you will soon realize that space is being created in your life for something new to emerge".

Eckhart Tolle

Three

The Future IS Now

FOR OVER TWENTY YEARS, I'VE been focused on helping business leaders and teams be future ready with a people first focus.

The "NextMapping" theme song title is, 'The Future is Now'.

For many people, focusing on the future can create major anxiety, while for others it's exciting and hopeful.

The truth is that the future IS now.

Everything we think and do in the now is creating the future.

In quantum theory, the past, present, and future are ALL happening at once in the now.

I've been a student of Eckhart Tolle's books and work for some time, and his philosophy of 'the power of now' is transformative.

As humans, we can get trapped in focusing on the past, which leads to depression. Conversely, if we are thinking too much about the future, we increase our stress and anxiety.

The antidote to the fixating on the past and the anticipatory fear of the future, is to practice being firmly rooted in 'the now'.

When the pandemic shutdown happened, we could all feel the frozen in time feeling. We were all forced to be with ourselves and our families during lockdown in a closed in environment.

In the lockdown environment 'gifts emerged' including:

We realized how distracted we had all become with 'busy' work.

We recognized that we were not present in our lives or with our families.

We began to value things that we had overlooked or taken for granted such as being in nature.

We began to play more board games and play outside.

We began to cook more home cooked nourishing meals.

We appreciated each other more deeply.

We focused more on our health and well-being.

We cared more for each other.

We went on a soul search.

We all got 'real' and 'more human'.

We became aware of how grateful we were for the simple things.

We realized that what really mattered was how we loved and live.

We faced the reality of our lives; what was working and what was not working and what needed to change.

The gifts listed above were all the result of a major disruption of the pandemic. Through major disruptions we all grew.

Exercise:

Take a pause here and think about and answer the following questions:

What is the biggest mindset shift you've made since the pandemic?

What are the changes you've made in your life and work?

What are you grateful for because of the pandemic?

The pandemic increased the awareness around the need for us to take inspired action on human rights issues. We have an opportunity now to help heal and to set new directions for a positive future for all humanity.

When we are fully present with reality, we do not look away at the challenging issues, we become present with what is happening in the now, we face it, and we decide how we can help.

Awareness of inequities and injustice is the first step. The next step is to not look away. Lastly, we acknowledge our part and act to be a part of the solutions.

The book is called super crucial 'human' because its crucial we become better humans.

Humans ARE the future, even in an automated and robotized future.

We are being called to be better and do better, AND we need to be better humans.

The societal unrest we are experiencing is due in part to polarity thinking by individuals. Polarity thinking by us as humans is when we hold firmly to a position, beliefs, or judgments, and we are attached to our 'viewpoint'.

When there are people with two opposite views at play it creates polarity (two opposites) and polarity thinking can lead to conflict and at its worst, potentially violence.

An example of polarity thinking could be that one person believes that the best way for business to thrive is for everyone to work in the office. Another person may believe that the best way for business to thrive is for everyone to work remotely.

The person who believes that everyone needs to work in the office is basing his or her belief of their own experience and bias that 'in person' is better. The person who believes that everyone needs to work remotely is basing his or her belief of their own experience and bias that 'virtual' is better.

When there is no compromise or give on either parties' viewpoints it creates polarity. Polarity creates tension. Polarity lies in the fixed mindset of each person for or against an issue.

Polarity thinking is a main cause of resistance to change.

When we elevate and raise our thinking to use the 'learn mindset' from the 'me to we' model, we can improve our ability to listen and seek to understand. Seeking to understand is the gateway to creative solutions.

We cannot avoid polarity thinking; however, we CAN become aware when we are stuck in it. We can also become aware when we witness it in other people. The opportunity is to help identify when we are in polarity thinking and then elevate our approach to ask questions and listen with empathy to find common ground.

A key factor in why we may get stuck in polarity thinking is unconscious bias. Using the polarity example of, 'in person' vs 'virtual' both the person who believes 'in person' is best AND the person who believes that 'virtual' is best has an unconscious bias. Each person is projecting what they think is right based on their own personal preference.

In each of their own minds they are right! However, polarity thinking can create an impasse when we do not want to hear or be open to an opposing opinion. You likely heard the term 'unconscious bias' in terms of diversity and inclusion. As humans, we are all biased.

Bias is a key component of creating polarity. In terms of diversity an example of unconscious bias is the denial of white privilege by a white person. If someone denies an issue it creates polarity. In other words, if someone doesn't see a problem because the situation benefits themselves unconscious bias is at play. We all have a heightened responsibility to be open and aware to the cultural issues and the societal issues happening in our communities and in the world.

As we move forward as humans, we need to become more aware of our biases and actively seek to acknowledge where our biases create polarity.

The Oxford dictionary defines unconscious bias as:

Any distortion of experience by an observer or reporter, of which they themselves are not aware.

In other words, it's called unconscious bias until we become 'conscious' of our bias. We must call out our own biases.

To be a better human, we all must be more aware of our thinking and how our thinking shapes our communication and behaviors.

The 'me to we' mindset model helps as an accountability tool to discover where we are stuck in our thinking. If we are in polarity thinking we are firmly in the 'personal' and 'blame' levels.

For example, if a person believes that working in person is the only way to work, and they used the mindset 'me to we' model to assess where they are, they will realize they are stuck in 'personal'. They are fixed in the belief that the way he or she does something is superior to everyone else's way of doing things.

The other bias that we can be unaware of in our thinking is 'confirmation bias'.

Confirmation bias is when we seek to find information that confirms our beliefs, position, or identity. Recently, I was on a virtual conference call with a group of senior leaders. We were discussing an event where I was to be the keynote speaker for their upcoming leadership conference.

One of the leaders on the committee asked me about research he had read that said virtual work was a temporary phenomenon, and that everyone would be going back in office. His comment was an example of confirmation bias. He had an unconscious bias that 'in person' is better. I honored the comment and acknowledged the research he was referring to. Then I shared counter research cited by numerous viable sources. I pointed out, in times of major change, we will operate from unconscious bias AND seek to confirm what we WANT to believe through confirmation bias. To his credit the leader agreed that it was his preference for everyone to go back to the office. The entire group recognized that these biases were at play throughout their leadership team and organization. They also recognized that both unconscious and confirmation biases in their culture were contributing factors overall to the companys struggle with change.

*"That's strange. I remember it differently, in a way that aligns
with my world view and casts me in a positive light."*

Unconscious and confirmation biases are prevalent in times
of uncertainty. These biases create discord and polarity.

Being a better human means we take full accountability for
our biases. Being accountable for our biases means we are
willing to be challenged in our thinking. We are willing to
change our mind.

We are willing to be present, aware, uncomfortable, and
accountable.

When we are firmly in the 'now', we can listen with our hearts.

When we are heart centered, we can shift from polarity (fear based) to integration (love based).

Integration/love is the evolutionary opportunity for us as humans now.

To become integrated, we must shift from polarity thinking to inclusive thinking.

Inclusive Thinking

When we use inclusive (head/heart) thinking, we are using the tools from the 'me to we' mindset model and the 'accept it, change it, leave it' model.

Rather than get stuck in polarity we

consistently seek to find what two opposites have in common.

Inclusive thinking is when we fully integrate logical head thinking with heart-centered thinking. We do not value head logic over heart, and we do not value heart over head logic.

One form of thinking is not better than the other (that would be polarity) both head and heart thinking is the way forward to creating a better future. Head/heart thinking is the pathway to being a better human.

Pre-pandemic many of us were valuing and operating from head thinking (logic) on its own.

Living through the pandemic has humanized us, opened our hearts, increased our compassion, made us feel vulnerable, and allowed us to become more authentic.

The pandemic itself has revealed many polarities in society including, politics, the virus and vaccines, black lives matter, gun control, women's rights and more. These issues have become heated and created massive upheaval. The upheaval of societal changes is necessary to bring greater awareness to the things that need to change. Polarity is a necessary step in our evolution towards being better humans. We are at an evolutionary growth opportunity to shift beyond polarity and elevate to integrated thinking and solutions.

We can choose to become fixed in a viewpoint that creates polarity.

We can choose to become flexible in our viewpoints, and practice inclusive thinking.

The only way we can be more flexible and inclusive in our viewpoints is to open ourselves to increase our 'heart centered' thinking.

Let's look at head centered thinking/heart centered thinking and the integration of both.

Head Centered	Heart Centered	Inclusive/Love
Logical	Emotional	Emotional intelligence
Structured	Creative	Design thinking
Practical	Out of the box	Creative solutions
Systematic	Organic	In the flow
Data	Anecdotal	Storyteller
Linear	Zigzag	Innovative

Looking at the above chart we can see that 'head centered' thinking has been highly valued over 'soft skills' or 'heart centered' thinking.

Inclusive head/heart thinking is an evolutionary opportunity for humankind.

Imagine if everyone in your family had high emotional intelligence.

Imagine if everyone in your community had high design thinking the ability to be creative AND take the practical actions to make a creative idea happen.

Imagine if everyone in your workplace operated with a focus on coming up with collaborative creative solutions.

Imagine how your life would be if you would be able to go through each day being 'in the flow' because you have mastered head/heart thinking.

Imagine that you could elevate your communication to be a storyteller who can weave both heartfelt anecdotal stories with research and facts.

Imagine our politics if everyone in government could shift to inclusive head/heart thinking!

Much of the future ready skills coaching I have been doing over the years has been to help leaders and team members be 'more human'. I can tell you that 99% of the time the challenges we face as humans are because we value 'logic' over 'emotions.'

Our very future requires us to get good at decoding the unique elements that make us human.

Robots cannot emote.

Robots cannot use 'heart thinking'.

Robots CAN help us automate the hard skills, master IQ and logic.

Robots/technology can be leveraged for good and to create the future of elevated human to human connections.

Humans MUST develop higher consciousness with heart/mind integration, it is super crucial for us to be better humans.

This IS the future.

The times when we focus on the differences between us as humans, we are in polarity thinking. The times when we focus on what we have 'in common' we are using integrative/ heart/love thinking.

What we ALL have in common regardless of race, gender, or culture is:

We are both human

We are both alive

We both have people who love us

We both want to do a good job

We both want to be seen and recognized

We both want to be successful

We both want to be good people

We both want to be happy

We both want to be healthy

We both have challenges

We both have our backstories

We both want to be loved

We both want to have a life

We both want to do rewarding work

We both have a variety of interests

We both live on the same planet

We both have done things we are not proud of

We both have done things we are very proud of

We have both made mistakes

We are both learning

ALL OF THE PEOPLE OF THE WORLD SEE THE SAME MOON

You get the idea 'the sheer act of seeking what's in common with another human leads to increased empathy, understanding and compassion.

"It's not greater technology but rather higher consciousness that gives us the power to work miracles."

Marianne Williamson

Four

What It Takes to Be a Better Human

WHAT WE NEED IN TODAY'S *complex and increasingly technology driven world is higher consciousness.*

Higher consciousness means we must elevate our minds to head/heart inclusive thinking. It's NOT easy, it takes focus, commitment, and a willingness to change.

A person's ability to master CHS (crucial human skills) will determine their future.

A few years ago, Jeffrey Weiner, the CEO of LinkedIn posted a comment saying, everyone needs more *soft skills*. In the article, Weiner went on to say how the skills people need to develop are those that have been undervalued by traditional workplaces. He went on to say that we have glorified IQ over EQ and it was time to change.

EQ is emotional intelligence which includes, empathy, humility, compassion kindness, communication, gratitude and more. I couldn't agree with him more, I have been writing and speaking about this for over two decades.

We need to change the term 'soft skills' to CRUCIAL HUMAN SKILLs!

By its very term soft skills denotes because of the word 'soft' that these skills are not as important as 'hard' skills. If you say to someone he or she needs more 'soft skills', they will often get defensive. Why? Because by its very term 'soft' people negate the importance of it. Technology skills are referred to as 'hard' skills and everyone values them because they are tactical and easily measured.

I posted a comment on Jeffrey's Linked In article saying, "while I agree completely with your article,

I am on a mission to change the term 'soft skills' to 'crucial human skills'.

Jeffrey Weiner liked my comment on LinkedIn, and my comment received a fair number of people agreeing with me. The more people that see soft skills as 'crucial' the faster we will all become better human beings. While it's a given that we all need to have technology skills we must have the human skills to leverage technology for good. In my experience with clients, many companies have based performance evaluations on hard and measurable skills. The companies that value crucial human skills measure them, include them in employee coaching and development, and expect teams to embody them as a cultural imperative.

Head/heart inclusive 'crucial human skills' are skills that need to be included in performance reviews, in coaching feedback, in our education system and in company values.

"The best advice I can give to a new teacher is to listen to your students with your ears and heart."

So, I repeat, I am on a mission to elevate our humanity by having us upskill our 'crucial human skills.'

There are many skills needed for us to be future ready. Technology aptitude is an absolute must. However, the people who will win now and, in the future, will also balance out technology skills and master these four crucial human skills.

These four skills require us to desire, focus and change our behaviors to be a better human.

4 Super Crucial Human Skills

Compassion

Conscious Communication

Creativity

Collaboration

The first super crucial human skill that is the foundation of being a better human is compassion.

Compassion

Many of us may believe we are compassionate. Many leaders will say they 'care' about their people, their employees, and their customers. Many organizations state 'we care' in their mission, vision, and values statements. However, saying 'we care' and walking the talk of 'we care' are two different things. A word that better encompasses the true meaning of 'care' is compassion.

As a skill compassion means:

A 'love' for people ' a strong compelling feeling of love for humanity as a whole.

A love for wanting to understand people better.

A love for doing what's right for people.

Empathy, ' the ability to empathize with peoples feelings, realities, pain and problems.

A few well-known examples of leaders with compassion in action includes the late Princess Diana when on April 19th, 1987, opened the first unit in the UK dedicated to treating people with HIV and AIDS. During her visit she shook the hands of an AIDS patient without wearing gloves and changed people's perception of the disease forever.

New Zealand's Prime Minister Jacinda Arden demonstrated empathy and compassion in leadership when she hosted a Facebook Live in March 2020 ahead of New Zealand's lockdown. Her personable approach along with her deep concern for her country's people was evident in her approach and communication.

Here in B.C. Canada where I live, Dr. Bonnie Henry leads with compassion. In all her communications she is calm, clear and acknowledges the challenges of each group throughout the pandemic. She's had tears in her eyes when speaking about the stress on health care workers and essential workers. Her compassionate approach helped us to hear and deal with the constant negative realities throughout the pandemic.

Her mantra is, 'we will get through this...together'.

Compassionate leaders put themselves in the shoes of others.

Where do you sit on the spectrum of having a love for people?

Do you genuinely care to understand where people are coming from?

Do you love for helping others to succeed?

Do you strive do what's right' for people?

Do you find people annoying?

Do you find yourself being cynical and judgmental of people?

Do you think people should just do their jobs?

People with compassion have a superpower. People trust you. People know you TRULY care

about them as a person, as a human being. People are loyal to you. People can hear your feedback because they know you are sincere in helping them to succeed.

The next element of compassion is empathy.

Empathy is not the same as sympathy.

Having empathy means we do not presume or assume we know what someone else is going through or feeling.

Sympathy is where we feel bad or sorry for someone.

Sympathy rather than empathy can come across as disingenuous. Sympathy separates us from the other person because we feel sorry for them, but we don't allow ourselves to be present with what they are truly going through.

Empathy builds a bridge of compassion because we are not afraid to be present with the uncomfortable feelings or emotions of the other person. We simply listen and create space for the other person to express themselves, we do not try to control the situation, make them feel better or diminish what they are feeling.

With empathy we can be present in the now, and we are able to be with someone's feelings, pain, realities, process, and problems.

When my husband had his health challenges, I found it challenging because I wanted to make it better. It was frustrating to be able to help my clients and yet I couldn't do anything to help my husband. Being empathetic meant I had to get comfortable feeling powerless. I realized I could do something, I could be present for him and his process and his experience without trying to change it, deny it or move on from it.

I've coached many leaders and team members to develop greater empathy. A leader may fear if he or she has empathy they will be viewed as 'soft' or 'weak'. The truth is a present, vulnerable, and empathetic leader has tremendous power. The power to positively influence, the power to build trust and the power to increase collaboration among teams.

Recently, I was coaching an executive leader around an issue with his team. A few team members had left his team to go work for other companies. Of his team of twenty, five of his team members had left to work at other organizations. In the leadership self-assessment that I had provided, this leader rated himself as an eight out of ten on empathy. We then compared his self-assessment with his team's assessment. His team rated him a five out of ten on empathy.

I then asked him why he thought his five team members had left for other organizations. His response was that it was out of his control, he couldn't compete with the money the team members had been offered. I asked how much more money they had been offered. He said it was not that much more than what they were already getting before they left.

I asked if his company would have matched the money if they had known the amounts, his response was yes. Then I asked if the company conducted exit interviews of the team members who had left. He said yes and the common reason given for leaving was for a better job and the second reason was that they did not feel supported by leadership.

At this point he got a bit defensive. He went on to outline all the ways he thought he WAS supportive. I paused to agree with him, that it is extremely challenging in today's reality to keep workers engaged. I then asked him if there was something he learned due to the five team members leaving. He said that he realized he could come across as too harsh and too focused on numbers and results.

Prior to being coached he had not linked leadership support to include empathy. One of the key leadership success factors increase loyalty and keep people is empathy. People need to feel heard, seen, valued, and supported by their leaders.

A compassionate empathetic leader has higher rates of employee retention. I asked the leader about how he would define his relationship with his team members. His response was he had good relationships with all his team members. I then asked if he saw signs of discontent in his weekly one on ones with his team members. His response was he did not do weekly one on ones with his team members he didn't have time. He also went on to say that at times he felt like a glorified babysitter. He admitted he felt his team members should be grateful to have a job and to work for such a great company.

And there it was......this leader was struggling with how to lead with compassion, he had become fixed in his leadership style, hardened to the targets, and he had been treating his team as a 'means to an end' i.e., / profits and cutting expenses.

Together we walked through the list of people who had left and wrote out the reasons why he thought each of them had left. I asked questions about what their personality type was, what was their personal situation and what did they like about their work prior to them leaving for another company. There were evident patterns as to why the team members had left. A pattern emerged that the leader did have weekly team meetings where he would lay out the goals and the expectations, however he did not engage the team in dialogue or questions. It was more of a one-way dialogue.

Another pattern was he was not having regular weekly one on ones to talk human to human or how the goals would affect each team member. His approach was 'one and done' ' one meeting, one message everyone should be on board. Finally, the last pattern was that when he did have conversations with each of his team members, he did not check in on how they were feeling, what they needed help with or ask for feedback on how he could be a better leader.

The bottom line in this case his lack of empathy and an attitude of 'people are disposable' led to this leader losing five team members over the course of a year. Now we might argue the reason the team members left is for other opportunities. While opportunity and money are factors in why people leave a job, they are not the only factors. Other important factors for workers to stay engaged include flexible work, the ability to work from home at least a few days a week, career growth, a career plan, feeling supported by their leader and feeling a sense of meaning and purpose.

I mentioned earlier we are in a worker's market and amid an era of the great resignation. People's work attitudes are shifting, 'how their leader make them feel' is at the top of their list when it comes to choosing where they work.

In a 2021 Talent Index survey over 5000 workers surveyed in the US and the UK about why they quit their jobs.

The top four reasons people quit their jobs in 2021:

Career growth opportunities

According to the Talent Index survey 83% of workers feel their leaders should be helping them to plan their career and future. 44% of workers stated their company provides a career path plan in place for their workers. In the above example the leader admitted he did not conduct regular discussions with team members about his or her future career opportunities. It is a crucial opportunity for leaders to help workers to plan for what's next in their career. In the past leaders would often think that 'having a job' was enough for workers. Today and in the future leaders need to be 'loving people' enough to want to help them plan for their future. An empathetic leader seeks to find out what each of their team members aspires to in their life and in their work.

Mental health a priority

The pandemic is still creating major stress for everyone. The constant influx of news about the virus, the new variants, the shutdowns, the travel advisories, has created increased tension. Leaders who show compassion for team members personal situations have higher rates of employee loyalty. Compassionate leaders make listening to their workers a priority. Compassionate leaders love people by listening, supporting, and providing resources to help their team members through their challenges. In the same Talent Index survey only 24% of those surveyed feel their leaders prioritized mental health with all workers.

Leaders who confuse worker contentment with loyalty

The leader example I gave above had confused his workers contentment with loyalty. In other words, in his opinion 'no news was good news'. He admitted that in the past, he thought having weekly one on one meetings took too much time. Today he regularly conducts weekly one on one meetings with is team members and his retention rate in the past six months is 100%. What he realized is he avoided having one on ones because he thought all his team members were doing fine. He even admitted that when he asked them how they were doing, and they said, 'fine' he took their answers literally. He now enjoys having the one on ones with his team members, he feels more connected and in tune with what each of his team members is feeling. A compassionate leader does not take a team member saying he or she is 'fine' at face value. A compassionate leader digs deeper, asks different questions, seeks to understand, and listens very closely.

Work-life balance

42% of those surveyed for the Talent Index said they want to continue with the flexible work gained during the pandemic. Prior to the pandemic the way offices and workplaces structure was based on the 9 to 5 model. Previously companies wanted 'bums in seats' to justify their office building and resisted remote working as an option for their workers. Now that workers have had a taste of remote work and work from anywhere there is no going back. Compassionate leaders understand their workers need for having a balanced life. A compassionate leader realizes that worker attitudes have shifted and there is an expectation of flex work, virtual work, and work from home. A compassionate leader will note the signs of fatigue in their workers before fatigue turns to burnout. A compassionate leader will notice the early signs of when a worker's performance is better or worse and will seek to understand what is going on in that workers' life to contribute to his or her performance.

Compassion fatigue

For some of you reading this whether you are a leader with a title or a leader without a title (which everyone is!) you may be suffering from compassion fatigue due to the additional stress and pressure of the pandemic. If you are in the front lines of the pandemic such as health care, community services, essential services, or retail you might feel you HAVE been compassionate to the point of exhaustion. Compassion as a crucial human skill is a skill we can manage with boundaries. The first person we need to be compassionate with is ourselves. The skill is to be compassionate, love people, be empathetic AND learn to discern boundaries within healthy compassion.

Having compassion does not mean we absolve other people of their responsibilities. Healthy compassion means we have a strong sense of self, a strong love for people and are empathetic while remaining focused on mutual accountability. Mutual accountability means I am responsible for my thoughts, feelings and behaviors AND you are responsible for YOUR thoughts, feelings, and behaviors. I can be compassionate with you and still know I cannot take on your challenges as mine. I know this is harder said than done. The person we need to be most compassionate towards is ourselves. Compassion with ourselves means we elevate our self-care so we can better resource ourselves.

We must remind ourselves we are human beings who are learning to 'know better' so we can continuously improve and 'do better'. I would say if you're suffering from compassion fatigue it is a sign for you to take a step back, to reset and to use resources to take care of yourself.

I've always had a strong love for people; however, I've not always been empathetic or compassionate. In my younger years I was keen on 'serving' people, and I always wanted to help people. However, in the past, I was impatient and irritated by people who didn't see things my way. As a socializer/driver personality I liked the social aspect of people, but I also wanted things done my way and right away. The people who could operate at my speed were my preferred people. Can you relate?

I've had great mentors throughout my entire career, and it wasn't until I had a few leaders point out my lack of compassion and empathy as a liability I became aware of it. I was fortunate in addition to pointing out my areas for improvement those same leaders pointed me in the direction of getting the training and support to help me be a better leader. Fast forward to twenty plus years of being a consultant/coach and I have developed compassion to be a key skill.

If compassion is the foundational super crucial human skill, then conscious communication would be the next one. In my case having a lack of compassion and empathy was because of my need for speed, results and efficiency. I had viewed compassion and empathy as taking up more time. Today, I know in the work I do compassion is the foundation to relational trust. Being sensitive to other people's feelings, emotions and needs doesn't slow things down. Being empathetic and compassionate creates more time as people can be more resourceful and productive when they are treated as a human being.

Conscious Communication

Communication is a necessary skill that leads to success. In the past baseline communication skills would include knowledge of assertive, passive aggressive, aggressive, and passive skills. Today and in the future, we need to elevate our communication skills and become masters of conscious communication.

The chart below helps to discern the different between baseline communication and conscious communication:

Baseline Communication Skills	Conscious Communication Skills
The ability to use assertive communication skills.	The 'love' (empathy/compassion) for wanting to connect and better understand others.
Knowing the attributes of aggressive communication.	
Knowing the attributes of passive-aggressive communication.	Know yours & others communication styles based on personality types.
Knowing the attributes of passive communication.	Know how to read the room and pick up on energetics of people.
Knowing your audience in verbal, written and text communication.	Seek to understand. multiple perspectives
The ability to listen and understand others.	Seek to listen with inclusive head/heart thinking
	Kind candor
	Set clear expectations aligned with personality

Many any of us have mastered baseline communication skills.

To be a better human we need to master conscious communication skills.

Knowing your communication style means you have likely completed one or more personality assessments. You have spent time on self-knowledge and understanding your communication preferences. For example, based on your personality style you know what your preferred form of communication, whether its text, to pick up the phone, send an email, have a virtual call, or talk in person. In addition to knowing your own personality style, because of your love for people, you have spent a large amount of time getting to learn more about other personality styles to better understand others. You have taken the time to learn the personality style of your family members, teammates, your boss, your suppliers, your trades, and your customers. In addition to learning what to look for in people's personality styles you have learned to adapt to other people's communication preferences. For example, your boss may be more of a thinker and prefers to have things laid out in writing and so rather than go and sit in your boss's office to have a chat (which might be what YOU prefer) you take the time to write it all out for your boss. Or even though you may prefer to have things in writing and your co-worker loves to talk things through you make the effort to be available to talk things through and then request a follow up in writing.

When we love people, we are eager to understand them. I truly believe in today's world we all need to think like psychologists or at the very least seek to have a better understanding of 'why' people think or do what they do. Understanding personality styles is one way of better understanding people. It's not about putting people in boxes or to create limited perspectives of a person. Rather, understanding personality styles is a usable framework that helps us to appreciate the differences among people. I find the personality styles framework extremely helpful for finding those things we as humans have 'in common'. In my previous books I have talked about the 4 D's: Driver/Dancer/Detailer/Deflector as personality types. There are a wide variety of tools (some of them free) available such as DISC, What's Your Color? Or

Myers Briggs that provide comprehensive insights into the personalities of people.

I recently worked with a team leader who was struggling with a team member who was very emotional. The team leader was a no-nonsense driver personality. The team member was an emotive deflector personality who would easily cry or get teary during a conversation. Once they each went through the personality assessments and shared their results with each other they instantly had a new level of understanding of each other. Once they gained a new level of understanding of each other, they were each better able to communicate and to not get triggered by behaviors they didn't understand. The driver personality wants to get things done quickly and efficiently, the deflector personality wants to feel and sense things before acting. The driver leader took the time to talk things through and to show more compassion. The deflector learned to not take it personally when the driver was in 'fast action' mode.

A conscious communicator knows how to 'read the room' and pick up on the energetics.

You've heard the phrase 'read the room' when someone blurts something out not at all in alignment with the vibe in the room. As a skill, reading the room means we must be present with the dynamics and different personalities in the room. When I am presenting to groups, I have developed the ability to think about what I am saying, seeing how it lands on a diverse group of people and then adapt to the nuances of their responses before speaking again. I'll give you an example. In March 2020, my last in person keynote event before the shutdown of the pandemic. It was for a group of police leaders and fire fighter leaders. My keynote was focused on the future of communities. I shared research on how the future of policing and fire fighters was going to be more focused on disaster relief, community support and social work. As I was sharing the research, I could sense the mostly male audience wasn't agreeing with the research. The research I share on 'future of all things' can cause some people to feel threatened and think, 'this will never happen' as a defense. I don't take it personally, its research based, I share the trends and patterns that point to the future.

I picked up on the energy of the audience's resistance to the research, I paused, I invited them to disagree with me via text message. I said, "if you think the research I am sharing is not going to happen, please text me'. I sensed the discomfort, spoke to the discomfort, and then invited them to disagree with me. I did receive many text messages from the audience and while on stage, I addressed their disagreements. I then went on to say we can either resist change or we can see the signs of upcoming change and adapt in advance. The energetics of the room shifted from resistance to curiosity and possibility.

The meeting organizer sent me a note saying they had never in their twenty years of running the conference seen so much interaction and participation in a keynote. They indicated they thought it was due to my invitation for the audience to disagree with me which they found refreshing.

The pandemic shut down happened the week after that keynote. The research I had shared had become real, police were helping with the shutdown and fire fighters were assisting the community with setting up Covid testing sites. The exact research I had shared had happened. I would like to believe that timing of my message helped them to cope better in some small way.

As a conscious communicator, our love for people supersedes our need to prove anything or to be right. We welcome disagreement, we welcome opposing views, we seek to influence not coerce.

Some tips on reading the energetics and reading a room are:

Be aware of your own energy you are bringing to the room, are you feeling confident and centered?

Tune into the energy of the room ' does the energy feel tense?

Does the energy of the room feel energized?

Think about who is going to be in the room if it's a planned meeting think about each of the individual personality types who will be in the meeting.

Think about the patterns of behavior of each person ' who is likely to disagree? Who is likely to be vocal? Who is likely to be onboard with you?

Be aware of your triggers, those things that can make you feel defensive. Who is likely to trigger you? Why?

Be aware of your filters (for example if you tend to blurt things out really work to hold this impulse in check) catch yourself before saying something that doesn't fit in with the discussion. Ask yourself, is what I am about to say relevant to the conversation? Is what I am about to say adding value?

Be prepared to interact and add value by preparing for the meeting and everyone's likely response in advance.

Be prepared to back up anything you share with research, anecdotal evidence, or examples.

During the meeting 'read the room' by intently watching people's responses if it's a virtual meeting look for people's cues on camera are they distracted? Are they doing something else? Do you sense someone wants to speak up?

Seek to Understand Multiple Perspectives

A conscious communicator, seeks to better understand where others are coming from. In basic communication we are often only able to see one or two perspectives at best. The one or two perspectives we see are our own and the other persons' perspective.

A conscious communicator elevates the ability to see things from multiple perspectives. Seeing things through a variety of lenses is a crucial human skills ability that when mastered can fast-forward projects, solve conflicts and build creative solutions.

For example, depending on what you do for work you may find yourself getting frustrated with a certain aspect of the work. Perhaps you are frustrated your co-workers don't seem to be working as hard as you do.

Or perhaps you get frustrated your senior level leaders aren't sharing information. Maybe your company is going through a massive upgrade of technology and there is lack of communication between IT and your department.

Regardless of the stressful situation, it is extremely helpful to elevate to multiple perspectives. In the example of you are frustrated your co-workers don't seem to be working as hard as you ' a single perspective would be its about you and your job and your work and how you perceive it. A dual perspective is you can see how you do your job and work AND you can see what your leader is doing to ensure the team all workers equally hard. A next level of perspective is you can see the dual perspectives AND you can also see from the perspective of the other workers situations, work styles, personality styles, the tools that the other works have access to, the skills that the other work may or may not have, and finally the lack of information you may have about the whole picture. A compassionate perspective is you would look more deeply at the circumstances your co-worker may be dealing with, which would help you to see the whole picture with a broader view.

We can gain multiple perspectives by asking empathetic questions, clarifying assumptions, and gathering input from others with different perspectives.

The 'me to we' model is an additional tool to help us to elevate to multiple perspectives. When we seek to understand multiple perspectives, we are operating from a 'we' mindset, and we can choose to consciously communicate from an elevated perspective vantage point.

Seek to listen with inclusive thinking

Elevating to multiple perspectives helps us to listen with an inclusive mindset. Remember an inclusive mindset is integrated head/heart thinking. We seek to find what we have in common with another person.

We seek to hear both the logic and the emotion of what is being said.

We seek to understand what the other person wants or expects from us.

We can better understand even though someone may be saying something illogical it's likely because they are feeling emotional.

We can then be present with the emotions and meet them there with empathy.

We can better understand when we are emotional it can appear illogical to the other person.

When we listen with our 'heart' we are listening for more than what is being said. We are using our intuition.

We have heightened intuition when we listen with inclusive thinking. Rather than listen with intent to respond, inclusive listening is listening with presence, with heart and letting the other person finish. Only when the other person has finished speaking can we listen and intuit what needs to be said next. It takes practice to listen with presence and inclusive thinking. You will find your communication will vastly improve with heightened awareness around head/heart inclusive listening.

In the exercises section I will give you some things to try to help to anchor this practice for you.

Kind Candor

Another aspect of being a conscious communicator is the ability to use kind candor. Candor on its own is easy for driver personality types where we can blurt, speak up and share the unfiltered truth.

My socializer/driver personality type means I had a problem in the past of bluntly speaking up or saying what I feel I did not have great control over my 'bluntness' filter.

Candor on its own can be refreshing and it can also be harmful. In my younger years, I used to believe when someone flinched with my candor it was because he or she couldn't handle the truth. When I learned more about conscious communication, I realized my need to blurt out the truth was more about me and my self-inflated ego than it was about helping the other person.

I was fortunate to have been given feedback by team members who told me I could get more 'flies with honey' with a kind candid approach. That's where I learned about the power of candor with empathy and compassion. I learned kind candor went a lot farther with people.

Kind candor can include tough love. It is the ability to be truly empathetic, caring and sensitive while being truthful and candid. At NextMapping, we have surveyed thousands over the years and when we asked workers what they most valued as a leadership skill by their leaders they said, "the ability to tell me the truth in a way that I can hear it, even if I don't want to hear it". That is kind candor.

The greatest leaders who have mastered their coaching skills have mastered the art of kind candor. I have been the lucky recipient of kind candor with several of my previous bosses throughout my career. When I was in my twenties, I had one boss tell me although I was excellent at giving feedback, I came across as too harsh. I had another boss tell me my ability to give observant feedback was excellent, however I needed to improve and use 'kind candor'.

I have been very fortunate throughout my career to have leadership coaches tell me if I could master empathy, I would be a master coach.

Now fast-forward to twenty + years later of having a consulting practice, I have been a consultant and coach to hundreds of clients and the feedback I receive is they truly appreciate my ability to show deep care while also sharing difficult insights and truths.

Recently I had a coach client who was going through a very difficult time with her family. Her husband had lost his brother suddenly, they had two small children who were having sleep issues and another family member had been diagnosed with Covid and was severely ill. In addition to the personal challenges, she was facing she was struggling with big changes in her role at work.

I felt deeply empathetic and emotional for the client. I could sense her pain and her feelings of despair. When she would talk, I would lean forward and listen intently, I listened by hearing the words as well as tuning in to the energetics of what she was sharing. I then asked her permission for me to share a few observations.

We had built trust over several coach sessions, and I had also set the expectations of the coaching process, including the use of kind candor. I shared I could feel her pain it was a tough time for her and I could not imagine the stress she must be enduring through these challenges. I paused. We both had tears in our eyes, I stopped talking, we both just sat with the energy of her challenges. Then I shared a few of the observations, one she was being extremely hard on herself. Two, she was trying to push through her pain, avoid it and keep going. I asked her if she had given herself time to grieve her brother or to ask for support. She had not. Lastly, with kind candor I asked her to think about what she could be doing to take care of herself, to give herself permission to grieve, and who she could ask for support. It was a sensitive, emotional, and challenging situation.

After that call, the client did take action, she set up grief counseling, set up daily rituals for self-care with her husband's help, and she asked her friends to help with play dates for the kids. In addition, she had a crucial conversation with her boss to share her personal struggles and to ask for support and understanding.

Kind candor is not meant to solve other people's problems. Kind candor is being present, attentive, asking thoughtful questions, while offering truthful insights (with permission).

I know I appreciate when people are candid, I find it refreshing and authentic. The key is a 'kindness' approach with the candidness.

The last key aspect of conscious communication is the ability to set clear expectations aligned with other people's personality styles.

In the current reality of increased stress, hybrid work environments and virtual teams there is a higher rate of miscommunication among people. A conscious communicator takes full responsibility for ensuring he or she has outlined expectations clearly and frequently. This applies to our personal relationships and our work relationships. Often, my clients' challenges are a result of not setting clear expectations.

Here are some guidelines to set clear expectations aligned with others personality styles:

Focus on the outcome you would like for example if you have a project you are leading at work what is the result you are aiming for?

Now, work backwards on your calendar to identify the steps of what needs to happen to get to the outcome.

Identify what you bring to the project what are your unique skills you bring?

Identify the personalities of the people who will be involved in the project ask yourself what are their strengths?

From there, set up a conversation with each of the stakeholders in the project.

Create a visual of what you expect as the outcome, use a slide or draw an image.

Clearly articulate what you envision and how you see the team getting there

Ask for the team's input do they see something you don't?

Create a step-by-step plan that identifies each person's role and expectations for their role.

Have a one-on-one meeting with each person involved ' speak in his or her personality language. i.e., / a driver type ' be direct and to the point, a socializer type make it fun for them, amiable type focus on their impact on the team, thinker type put everything in writing.

The above steps can be used in any scenario and has helps immensely in personal relationships as well. A lot of times we will make assumptions about people. When we assume we are not being empathetic or compassionate, instead we are focused on a single perspective, our own.

Setting clear expectations may sound like a lot of work, I have found as you master it as a daily skill it becomes an innate skill that ends up saving you a lot of time and grief in the end.

As you can see there are distinctive differences between basic communication skills and conscious communication skills. While basic communication is considered a nice to have, conscious communication is a need to have as we strive to be better humans.

Creativity

The next super crucial human skill we need to elevate is our creativity.

Creativity is such a broad term. Often, we equate creativity to being artistic. There is a myriad of ways to be creative. When you cook a meal and follow a recipe you are being creative. When you play a game with your child or grandchild you are being creative. The times where you solve problems on the fly, you are being creative.

As a human skill, creativity is a source of inspiration and energy.

The components of creativity I believe are the biggest areas for opportunity for us are curiosity and asking questions.

Creativity is not just for certain people. People can feel they don't know how to be creative or it isn't their job to be creative. Recently I worked with a Japanese client in the pharmaceutical industry. I worked with their leadership team on a series of virtual meetings where the focus was on innovation and creativity. I met with the CEO to discuss the outcomes and to prepare the seminars prior to the events. When I asked him his main outcome, he wanted from the virtual events he said he wanted *everyone* to feel inspired and responsible for being creative.

This company was already highly innovative and in fact had won many innovation awards in Japan. However, as a true innovator the CEO wanted the shift of responsibility for innovation from their innovation lab to all workers.

I had conducted a survey sent to all the leaders who would be participating in the virtual events asking for their thoughts on creativity. For the most part, the consensus from the survey responses was the leaders didn't know how to be creative in their daily work, nor did they know how to help their employees be more creative.

In the virtual event I shared the barriers to creativity such as the fear of disagreeing or the need to support group think. This created a larger dialogue around the company culture that supports creativity in the workplace.

The goal for us is to build our 'real time' creativity muscles. You are likely already doing this to some degree. As we build our compassion and seek to see and find things in common our creativity naturally increases.

Some ways to build our daily real time creativity is to consistently ask ourselves a few questions:

Is there something else or someone else I could consider with this challenge/situation/ person who could add insight?

What are the things I can see in common with this challenge/situation/person and other challenges/situations/people from the past?

What are the patterns with this challenge/situation/person that have happened repeatedly? Why? What is a new way to approach this?

Asking questions is a sign of intelligence and to ask questions is to seek to understand. I believe there is no such thing as a silly question, and I also believe you cannot ask too many questions. Early in my leadership career, I used to get triggered by people who asked a lot of questions. At the time I believed allowing a lot of questions would slow me down. Or I would feel defensive because I felt the person who asked me a lot of questions didn't trust me. Today, I welcome and enjoy a lot of questions. I can tell you every single time someone asks a question it reveals something I need to be reminded of or I did not consider. Or the questions confirm the research and gets us all on the same page. In order to ask great questions we have to have heightened curiosity.

Curiosity

When we are curious, we are in the 'learn' mindset I mentioned earlier from the me to we model.

Being curious means we are open-minded.

Being curious means we seek to learn new things.

Being curious means having a sense of wonder.

Being curious means being more playful.

Being curious means we are less serious.

Being curious means we seek to understand.

Curiosity is the key to being creative. The next time you find yourself feeling irritated try being curious as to why. Ask yourself the following questions:

Why is this irritating me?

What is irritating me?

How do I behave when I am irritated?

Do I like who I become when I am irritated?

Curiosity is a way of looking at the world and at everything. In his book, "How to Think Like Leonardo DaVinci", author Michael Gelb shared how deeply curious Da Vinci was.

Da Vinci would go for daily walks and while walking he was intently curious about everything he saw. He would ask himself questions such as:

How does a bird fly?

How could humans fly?

What makes animals hibernate?

How to mother animals take care of their babies?

What can animals teach us about life?

Most of Da Vinci's inventions were created based on his curiosity around what things that seemed to be opposites had in common. For example, when inventing flying machines, he asked what birds and humans had in common. He noted both birds and humans had appendages. Birds had wings ' humans had arms. Both had two feet. Both had eyes. From there he was able to take his curiosity of 'how' a bird flew and link that to creating wings on a machine.

We are now living in a time when we are on the precipice of a post pandemic renaissance. The fast pace of change in the last decade including the past few years of the pandemic have accelerated the pace of innovation.

We are going to experience more innovations in our life and work in the next few years than we have seen in the previous decade.

However, creativity is not something found outside of ourselves.

My granddaughter Olive is six years old and since she came along, I have learned a lot from her. She has taught me to be present, to look at the world through her young eyes. Olive is a talker, and she asks endless questions, and I love it!

Being a grandparent has definitely expanded my creativity!

Creativity is NOT something some people have, and others do not. Creativity arises from an open mind and from deep curiosity.

Another key element of creativity is the ability to see conflict or confrontation as an opportunity. Often the most innovative ideas have come from a group of people with diverse and opposing views coming at a problem from a multitude of angles.

As human beings the better we get at handling confrontation the better we are at being a better human. Confrontational tolerance is the ability to stay present and calm while listening with deep presence and not taking opposing views personally.

Having the ability to see conflict as an opportunity for us to learn and create is a superpower. One strategy to build your confrontational tolerance is the 'finding things in common' exercise daily. In addition, here are the questions we can ask ourselves when faced with confrontation:

What is my default behavior when someone confronts me? i.e., /do I become aggressive, passive or passive aggressive?

Is there some truth to the other person's perception or problem?

What is behind or beneath the confrontation? i.e., /what else is going on with the person or is something else triggering him or her?

Mastering the first three super crucial human skills will make life easier and less stressful. And to be a true collaborator we must master the ability to work in a team, with a team and to share energy, knowledge and power.

Collaboration

In 2021, we saw the rise of the hybrid workplace (in office & remote) after most of 2020 where most of us were working remotely. Depending on the nature of the work some workers were in office or on site throughout the entire pandemic. Other workers were able to work primarily remote due to the nature of their work. In Fall of 2021, many companies implemented a hybrid working structure for their company. Then with the rise of Omicron many of us went back to fully virtual.

Working remotely or working hybrid has created team challenges. Depending on the technology in place some workers were able to seamlessly move their work to work from anywhere. Other companies where they had not yet upgraded their technology solutions struggled.

Many leaders were and are challenged with onboarding workers remotely or training workers remotely. A leadership survey we conducted in December 2021 indicated many leaders were struggling with keeping workers engaged in a hybrid workplace.

The shift from a traditional work environment to hybrid or fully remote has been a massive change which has impacted everyone.

The people who are going to thrive now and into the future are those who able to collaborate at high levels in a hybrid reality. The attributes of a person who is a master collaborator are:

Consistently has a 'share' mindset as outlined in the 'me to we' model.

Consistently seeks to learn and is highly curious.

Seeks to gather insights and input from others to make the best decisions.

Has high level of self-awareness (personality style/communication style) and knows how others can perceive him or her.

Has developed confrontational tolerance, the ability to be with diverse and opposing opinions without taking it personally.

Sees technology/robots/AI as a co-worker and a collaboration tool.

Has such high self-esteem he or she doesn't take feedback defensively or personally.

Views other perspectives as highly valuable to overall success of work.

Consistently seeks to add value by sharing knowledge and resources.

Takes the time to help others learn on the fly i.e., /how to use features in Zoom on a group call.

Does not focus on job titles or hierarchy ' sees everyone as important.

Enjoys seeing others succeed beyond themselves and surpass them in their career success.

Consistently checks himself or herself for biases when interacting with others.

Seeks opportunities to increase diversity within the team.

Values the results of a team collaborative effort over self-recognition or self-promotion.

Communicates consciously and ensures he or she factors in other personalities when writing emails, texting, in person or virtual.

Is 'woke' to social matters and is comfortable with all gender pronouns, aware of and sensitive to cultural events/holidays/appropriations.

Welcomes disagreement knowing it leads to better dialogue and creative solutions.

Loves people as human beings ' loves that people are different and diverse ' loves that we are all learning and growing as humans.

Crucial Human Skills Exercises

I am a big believer in micro learning and applying what we learn in small doses daily. The reality is when we listen to a keynote or when we read a book, rarely are we taking massive action right afterwards. If I think of all the people I have learned from over the years, I have taken bits and pieces from every book I have read and every person I heard speak. In my research most people don't even finish a book! In fact, when I surveyed several clients most said they choose sections of a book and read those but rarely the entire book. We are all working hard, and we have a lot on the go. We only set ourselves up for failure when we add another burden of having to commit to something that adds to our already overloaded workload. That's why this list of exercises is just a list. I want you to treat this list as something you will come back to as you feel inspired, not something you have to tackle all at once.

In my previous book, "NextMapping ' Anticipate, Navigate and Create The Future of Work" I wrote a companion workbook which was published a year after the original book came out. The companion workbook provides questions to help better understand your mindset about change and the future.

In this book, I wanted to include the exercises so you had everything you needed in one place.

Instructions for the exercises:

Read through all the exercises.

Choose ONE exercise that inspires you and commit to it for a thirty-day period of small daily micro actions.

Set a goal through an online reminder such as futureme.org so you automate a reminder to yourself of your goal.

Set visual reminders for you to act with your micro actions with either a paper sticky note, an online sticky note, an alarm or a reminder.

Once you complete the 30-day cycle debrief your progress, celebrate your wins, and share your wins with others.

Choose another exercise from the list and start at step one.

Exercise #1 Love People Perspectives Exercise

When you read the opening chapter of this book with the focus on, 'love people' as it relates to the future of humanity what were your thoughts?

Do you struggle with the concept of 'love people'? Why?

When you think about the future of humanity do you agree with the vision I shared? Why? Why not?

When you think about where we are now as a society do you think we are moving in the right direction? Why?

Do you find it difficult to 'love people' because you find yourself defaulting to judgement? Why?

Set yourself a daily 'love people' perspectives exercise. Set a reminder for you to do this five-minute activity every day.

Observe your thoughts and reactions to people during a meeting. Notice your thoughts about certain individuals. Are you judging? Are you assuming? Are you thinking negative thoughts about individuals?

Focus on your observations and try not to make yourself feel bad about your observations. Simply 'notice' your thoughts when interacting with different people.

Lastly, focus on one thing you appreciate about each individual you interact with, perhaps you appreciate someone's candor, or you appreciate someone's ability to be diplomatic etc. Aim to practice this exercise daily.

Exercise #2 Your View of The Future of Humanity

Take a few moments to review the 'future of humanity' predictions in Chapter One.

Are you an optimist? Why?

Which of the predictions resonate with you? Why?

Which of the predictions do you disagree with? Why?

When you look at your background and upbringing what are the beliefs you grew up with about life in general?

Who was your biggest influencer or who shaped your values when you were growing up?

What do you value the most? Make a list of 4 values IE/ connection, freedom, trust etc.

How much time do you spend reading or watching the 'negative' news?

Go through your Instagram and follow positive hashtags such as #goodnews #goodnewsmovement #positivenews

Do a 'feed cleanse' with your social media and unfollow or mute anyone or any group that perpetuates negative information.

Have a conversation at your dinner table or at mealtime with family members about what they think the future of humanity looks like.

Stay curious and open during the dialogue.

Think about your family, which elements of the future of families resonated with you?

What changes have you and your family made since the beginning of the pandemic? Why?

Exercise #3 Existential Questions

For this exercise make space for yourself where you can be alone and contemplate and journal your responses to the following questions. It's even better if you can meditate before answering or take a few moments of deep breaths prior to answering.

What is most important to me at this stage of my life?

What are my priorities?

What do I value?

Why do I work where I work?

How much work is too much work?

How much money is enough money?

What is the impact of my work on my family?

Am I compensated fairly for my work?

How do I want to be remembered?

What would it look like to live my best life?

What's best for my family?

What are my beliefs?

What activities feed my soul?

Am I doing what I love?

Who am I?

Once you have answered each of these questions, review your answers, what is the theme you see? Do you get a sense of a specific action you need to take because of your answers?

Exercise #4 A Learning Mindset

In Chapter Two the focus is on a 'learn' mindset and I asked you to pause and review our lessons learned since the pandemic.

Some lessons learned because of the pandemic include:

We learned we have absolutely zero control over many things

We learned we have full control over our thoughts and behaviors

We learned we could work remotely and virtually

We learned we could spend more time with family

We learned to commute for the sake of commuting seems quite silly now

We learned we are all human beings

We learned here are major inequities among us

We learned we need to be better humans

We learned a worker shortage means we NEED humans more than ever

We learned we need to be more empathetic

We learned we need to be more tolerant

We learned we need to be more flexible

We learned life is too short

We learned to deeply value who and what we love most

We learned bad things happen and the only thing we can control when they happen is our response to those things

We learned when things are hard, at the same time many new things and improvements are created

We learned love is an action, and we all feel our best when we take loving action

What else?

Exercise:

Take a pause here to sit with the above list, and then add what you have learned in the past few years.

How did what you learn help you make some life changes?

Exercise #5 Me to We Model in Action

Review the questions below:

What do I value the most, and are my actions aligned with what I value?

Why do I take it personally when things happen out of my control?

Who and what do I blame for my stress?

Why do I believe I need to work so hard and therefore I am burning myself out?

What is my true definition of wealth?

What do I want my legacy to be?

What makes me feel my most peaceful and relaxed?

What's best for me and my family?

How much money is enough money?

How can I share what I am learning to help others?

Review the 'me to we' model outlined in this book ' honestly answer the following question, "Where do I spend MOST of my time on the 'me to we' model. For example, if you admit you are in 'personal' or 'blame' most of the time then your goal is to set a daily practice of asking yourself, "What can I learn from this situation or challenge?"

Using a notes app or journal what you are learning. There will be times when it will be very difficult to admit you are learning anything and that's OK. The goal is to practice the question of "what I can learn" as a daily habit. If you answer you are in the 'learn' mindset most of the time, then your goal is to elevate to 'share' mindset daily. Your daily practice will be to ask yourself, "how can I share what I know and help people grow?" Again, keep track of your daily progress ' you could even use your voice app if that's easier too.

Make a visual reminder of your question so its top of mind. Whether that's a sticky note on your monitor, or it's a screen saver or it's a reminder you need to create a way of visually reminding yourself of your goal. If in reviewing the 'me to we model' you feel you are in the 'share' mindset most of the time then your daily practice is to ask yourself, "what is my proof I am operating from a 'share' mindset?". Keep track of the 'wins' within your life, team, department or company as a result of your 'share' mindset. For example, you will know you are consistently coming from a 'share' mindset because your team is fully autonomous. Your team is fully engaged. Your co-workers trust you and you inspire them daily. Your team is succeeding in reaching targets. You enjoy high levels of retention in your teams. Your team is highly collaborative. You invest considerable time on knowledge transfer to help your team, co-workers, and boss to know what you know. Track your wins to take note of the 'learnings' along your journey of consistently sharing.

Exercise #6 Accept It, Change It, Leave It Model

For every choice there is a consequence. For every action there is a reaction.

Think of a challenging situation you are in now and you would like to change.

It can be personal or work or relational.

Now ask yourself the following questions:

Can I accept the person and the situation as it is? In other words, can I just let it go and relax into the reality this person or situation is never going to change? (This means you stop bitching, whining, talking about or moaning about the person or the situation ' you LET IT GO.)

When you are having trouble accepting your challenging situation then it's a sign something must change. Often, we want to the other person to change or take the lead, however the 'change it' choice is about what YOU are willing to change. Ask yourself the following questions:

Did I try to approach this person or situation with a new approach?

How can I communicate in a way the other person will really 'get' what I am saying?

What can I read, listen to, or watch to help me shift my perspective?

Who can I ask for support to help me make the necessary changes?

Give yourself a time frame for 'change' to happen. For example, if the challenging situation does not shift after you make every effort to change in 90 days then what will you do next?

Does this situation require you to 'leave it'? In other words, did you do everything humanly possible to make a positive change?

Did you deeply consider the consequences of the 'leave it' choice? (In other words, wherever we go, there we are!)

Before you make the leave it choice did you ask for help?

Before you make the leave it choice did you communicate your true feelings about the situation?

Before you make the leave it choice did you envision what the potential outcomes may be of your choice?

If you do make the 'leave it' choice, what did you learn from the challenging situation or person?

What will you differently in the new place you are heading to?

What will you do differently when you are faced with a similar challenge in the future?

Exercise #7 Being Present with Now

In this book I shared the past/present/future are really all happening at once if you look at time as being influenced by the past, while we live in the now and while we envision the future.

Take the time to reflect on these questions:

Do I spend most of my time thinking about the past and how I wish things would go back to the way they were?

Do I spend most of my time thinking about the future and worrying about where things are going?

How does it make me feel when I fixate on the past or when I focus on the future?

What are the activities I do to help me stay present? i.e./ meditation, nature walks, listen to music, watch inspiring videos, play with kids/grandkids.

What happens to my stress levels when I find myself focused on the past or future?

What happens to my stress levels when I spend more time being present?

How do I show up in my family, in my life or at my work when I am stressed?

How do I show up in my family, in my life or at my work when I am present, calm and centered?

Who can I reach out to for support/help/dialogue to help me stay committed to being present?

Once you've reflected on these questions make a commitment of one or two daily actions to will help you to stay present. For example, you will carve out 10 minutes of every day to practice mindfulness. Or you will schedule a nature walk during your lunch every day. Or you will seek out videos that make you smile or laugh once or twice throughout the day.

We can't be our best human selves unless we take control of our own mental well-being.

I think we can agree throughout the pandemic we had zero control over many things. This caused many of us to feel trapped, isolated, frustrated, and angry.

The only thing we can control is our mindset and our behaviors throughout any disruption of any kind. No one is going to do this for us. If we practice self-love, we honor our need for regular 'time-outs' and it helps us to be present, calm and centered.

The more centered we can be the better of a human we can be. We can be our best selves when we prioritize our own well-being. You've heard the saying, 'fill your own cup first' or 'put your own mask on first', it is imperative we value ourselves, so we can then share with others at the highest level.

Exercise #8 Inclusive Head/Heart Thinking

In this book I talked about one of the biggest causes of resistance to change is 'polarity thinking' as well as unconscious and confirmation 'biases. In the previous exercise I had you focus on how to be more present and take care of your own well-being. It is very difficult to practice inclusive thinking if we are not being present. Read through and contemplate the following questions:

Where do I get trapped in polarity thinking where I am fixed on a position around a topic? i.e., /I stubbornly believe something to be true and am unwilling to listen to other viewpoints

What are some of my unconscious biases? i.e. / gender beliefs/ cultural beliefs

What are some of my confirmation biases? For example, do I only seek news or information that confirms what I believe, or do I seek out opposing viewpoints to balance my overall opinions?

Do I value logic over emotions? Why?

Do I value emotions over logic? Why?

In what ways do I think I practice inclusive thinking most of the time?

Set yourself a daily practice of seeking to find things in common. When going for walks look at everything you see and ask yourself what is in common. For example, what does a bird and a tree have in common?

Exercise #9 Super Crucial Human Skills

As outlined in this book there are four super crucial human skills we need to master to be a better human being.

Review the four super crucial human skills below and rate yourself on a scale of one to ten with ten being high on each skill.

Compassion

1   2   3   4   5   6   7   8   9   10

Need to work on   Average   Mastery

Conscious Communication

1   2   3   4   5   6   7   8   9   10

Need to work on   Average   Mastery

Creativity

1   2   3   4   5   6   7   8   9   10

Need to work on   Average   Mastery

Collaboration

| 1 | 2 | 3 | | 4 | 5 | 6 | 7 | 8 | 9 | 10 |

Need to work on   Average   Mastery

Now identify the skill you rated yourself as your lowest.

Next, set a thirty-day goal of how much you want to improve this skill, for example if you rated yourself a five you want to be a seven in thirty days.

Lastly set micro daily actions of intent to improve, for example you want to be more compassionate, so you are going to take a free online EQ (emotional intelligence) quiz to identify where you are. Or you are going to take five minutes a day to talk to ask each team member how they are personally doing.

Exercise # 10 ' Human Connections

Being a better human being means we are willing to take full accountability for how we communicate. Take a moment to review the list below of the conscious communication skills.

Conscious Communication Skills

The 'love' for wanting to connect and better understand others.

Know yours & others communication styles based on personality types.

Know how to read the room and pick up on energetics of people.

Seek to understand. multiple perspectives

Seek to listen with inclusive head/heart thinking

Kind candor

Set clear expectations aligned with personality

Which of the elements in the list do you think is your area for opportunity?

Again, select one item from the list and make a thirty-day commitment to get better at with the conscious communication item. For example, perhaps you feel you want to master the ability to understand personalities. Your micro actions would be to review your own personality assessment or take a new personality assessment. Another action item could be to list out your family members and identify each of their personality types. Or you could list your co-workers and identify each of their personality types.

It is my sincere wish you gained insights, ideas and aha's about the need for us to be better humans.

My work over the years has always been focused on people, how we can grow and evolve.

I am on this journey with you, writing this book caused me to self assess and hold myself accountable at a higher level to being a better human.

This book is aspirational, and I hope inspirational - if we all WANT to be better humans then our positive future is guaranteed.

I wish you health, well-being, peace, and abundance in your future.

With love,

Cheryl

Resources

Nextmapping.com/microlearning

Abundance: The Future is Better Than You Think by Peter Diamandis

How to Think Like Leonardo Da Vinci by Michael Gelb

Loving What Is by Byron Katie

The Power of Now by Eckhart Tolle

Headspace Meditation App

Calm Meditation App

Synctuition App

Crucial Conversations by Joseph Grenny

Human Hacking by Christopher Hadnagy

Untamed by Glennon Doyle

Atlas of the Heart by Brene Brown

General Magic Documentary with Marc Porat

Other books by Cheryl Cran

NextMapping ' Anticipate, Navigate and Create the Future of Work

The Art of Change Leadership ' Driving Transformation in a Fast-Paced World.

Index

Printed in the United States
by Baker & Taylor Publisher Services